Praise for *Love, Mrs. Euker*

"This memoir is an honest and authentic love letter from a master teacher to her fellow teachers."

—**Jack Canfield,** *Co-author of Chicken Soup for the Teacher's Soul*

"I've often said there is nothing better than a good teacher. Thanks, Susan Euker, for confirming me."

—**Jerry Spinelli,** Newbery Award winner: *Maniac Magee, Stargirl*

"I am delighted that my book Reviving Ophelia inspired Susan Euker to create an Ophelia Club at her school and serve as an empowering leader of girls. Her resilience in the face of cancer and her love of her students are inspiring."

—**Mary Pipher**, author, *Reviving Ophelia,* and *Women Rowing North: Navigating Life's Currents and Flourishing as We Age*

"Susan is of that special breed of educator who when asked, 'What do you teach,' would answer 'I teach students.' Her anticipation and eagerness to learn was so joy-filled, and her apprehension about returning to the classroom brimming with such excitement, it was as if she couldn't wait to open a gift... and what a gift she was."

—**Barbara Sullivan,** Drug-free facilitator; Supervisor of Health Education, Baltimore County Public Schools

"Consider reading this memoir if you are entertained and inspired by the authenticity, humor and the joy of teaching. Definitely read this memoir if you are drawn to the culture clash of a glass-half-full teacher as she takes on the dim world of teenage angst. Spoiler alert: the result is a strengthening of the teacher-student bond in unsuspecting and delightful ways."

—**Alex Allman,** Principal, Offit-Kurman Attorneys

"A love letter to teaching, Love Mrs. Euker shares frustrations, joys and hope. As one of her former teachers, like her, I honor with pride and grit and success that underline my 'Susan the student's' tales of life in the classroom."

—**Dr. Susan Radius**, Professor Emeritus, Towson University

"Inspiring and warm classroom stories as seen through the eyes and heart of Mrs. Euker, who never forgot what it was like to be on the other side of the desk."

—**Alicia Ruppersberger,** Hereford High Family Studies Department Chairperson, Baltimore County Public Schools

"In a time when teachers are so frequently maligned, these remembrances demonstrate the pivotal role that caring teachers play in the development of young adults. Additionally, this memoir not only speaks to the challenges, but also to the joys and sorrows of teaching."

—**Carolyn Fucile,** History Department Chairperson and Advanced Placement coordinator, Hereford High School. Baltimore County Public Schools

"A former co-worker would often voice, 'the best professional development is good hiring.' I couldn't agree more heartily. Having the right people working directly with students and dare I say, 'loving them,' is always the best choice. Susan Euker certainly fit the bill. Her reflections of high school exchanges are refreshing and send an accurate and powerful message to any naysayers who attempt to vilify youth. Mrs. Euker provides an affirming glimpse inside a most noble profession.

—**Michael Thatcher,** Director of Special Education, Harford County Public Schools

"As a former teacher, assistant principal and presently principal at Hereford High School, I have often thought to myself, 'I should write a book and tell the world what goes on around here.' Well, Susan Euker has done just that. Inspired by the memories she captured over twenty years at Hereford, she's put together a well-written and honest collection of stories that chronicles her career working with teenagers, focusing on what she learned about them and more importantly, what she learned about herself."

—**Louis J. Jira,** Principal, Hereford High School

"One word describes my memories of Mrs. Euker: 'IALAC' (I am Loveable and Capable). She was the first person on this earth that told me I was worth something, even when I didn't believe it about myself. I'm so grateful that God put her on my path."

—**Stacey Egerton Davis,** Senior Vice President, Business Development FinPay

"Full of honesty, humility, empathy, enthusiasm and strength, as she has brought to every relationship and endeavor. She takes you on a journey, her journey, with such ease and insight that it is easy to understand why all who have known her love Mrs. Euker.

—**Mary Kellam,** Lead Business Process Engineer at Highmark Medicaid Business Unit

Dec 6, 2020

Cathy,

I hope you enjoy reading my memoirs as much as I enjoyed writing them.

I wish you and Brendon, Eli and Mira joy and health in 2021.

maybe a vaccine in 2021?!

Love,
Susan

LOVE, MRS. EUKER

Reflections on a Career in the Classroom

"If some students are unresponsive, maybe you can't teach them yet, but you can love them. And, if you love them today, maybe you can teach them tomorrow."

Jeffery R. Holland

Susan Cunningham Euker

Print ISBN: 978-1-09833-061-3

eBook ISBN: 978-1-09833-062-0

A version of the story, *TJ, Learning a Lesson* previously appeared in *Chicken Soup for the Soul* and *Heart at Work*. It was also printed in *Reader's Digest, The Baltimore Sun* and *The Los Angeles Times*.

Photographs, unless otherwise identified, are from the author's private collection.

Printed in the United States of America

Jacket design by Marie Lanser Beck

Author photograph: Lisa Gerber Studios

Graphic Designs: Mykerria McNeill

Formatting: Katharine Euker Rinehart

To my husband, Carl, who was there for it all.

June 15, 1941-April 11, 2019

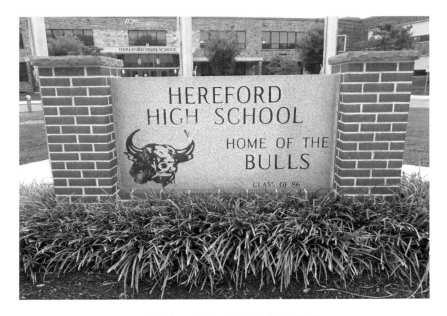

NOTE TO READERS

Out of deep respect for my colleagues and students at Hereford High School in most cases names, and occasionally gender, have been changed to protect the privacy of individuals mentioned in these stories.

The issues and themes I address in these reflections represent my personal experiences from more than twenty years in public school classrooms and are presented here as a tribute to teachers and students everywhere who are engaged in the noble process of education.

Susan Cunningham Euker

SYNOPSIS

Love, Mrs. Euker is a series of vignettes written by a 40-year-old former teacher who returns to the classroom after ten years of retirement, leaving the calm and comfort of her well-ordered suburban life as a wife and mother for the wilds of a modern blackboard jungle. While she aspired to have a positive influence on her students, what she didn't foresee was the unexpected impact returning to teaching would have on her.

In the true spirit of coddiwompling defined as traveling in a purposeful manner towards a vague destination, this Baltimore-based schoolteacher left her domestic cocoon and journeyed headlong into an unforeseen and unsettling future. While her family remained her central focus, she discovered a different dimension to her life, and in teaching teenagers, learned much about herself.

Experience the joys and heartbreak of a life-changing career in education as you stand in a teacher's shoes as she cheers her students' success, grieves over lives interrupted, and experiences the challenge and rewards of preparing young people for an uncharted future.

With wit, hard-earned wisdom and confessed foibles here and there, this veteran teacher presents a candid, insightful perspective of a career in education in all its tedium and shining moments of glory. In her account of twenty years of coaching, instructing, guiding and counseling students, live through the triumph and tears as she recounts her "purposeful journey towards a vague destination."

In this tribute to her former students at Hereford High School in suburban Baltimore, she writes for everyone who has ever sat in a classroom, or held a piece of chalk in their hand, or dreamed of inspiring the future.

This is a love letter to teachers and their students everywhere.

ACKNOWLEDGEMENTS

While travelers often journey alone, this coddiwompling took a village. Villagers are caretakers of memories who give generously of their time and talent as stories unfold. This memoir of my years in teaching required the dedication of countless hearts and hands from my village. My *vague destination* has been realized, and each of you has helped guide my uncertain footsteps.

To the Euker family, my husband, Carl, my children, Katharine, Stephanie, Keith and Carrie, and my grandchildren, Hannah, Ethan, Abby, Carson, Sadie and Bear, you have been my devoted cheerleaders, reminding your Mimi that she had something important to say.

Thank you, Abafamadie.

To my sisters, Marjie Poffel and Lynne Cunningham, who blew air back in my sails when there was none, your energy refilled my mainsail and directed me home.

Mom and Dad are smiling.

To my Hereford High School teaching colleagues, Alicia Ruppersberger, Carolyn Fucile and Denise Butcher, who were there with me in the classroom, the office and during pep rallies, you know these stories as well as I. Thank you for your academic and editing expertise.

We had a great ride.

To Mrs. Machala's eleventh grade Advanced Placement U.S. History classes, your insights, suggestions and cautions were significant to the content of the stories included by the author.

Your voices were heard.

To my friends, Judy and Wayne Carmen, Dale and Betsy Smith, Abby Praglowski, Dr. Liz Berquist, Brianne Duval Grill, Hannah Rinehart, Gail Huber, Mary Kellam and Joyce White, your patient reading and honest critique of my work, helped me pen my stories more completely.

Thank you for your time.

To all of the innocent but willing bystanders, who were buttonholed as I verbally recalled and sometimes tediously rehashed my stories, our chinwags were invaluable.

Thank you for staying.

And finally, special thanks, to my editor, Marie Lanser Beck, who believed my coddiwompling was worth sharing, and who shepherded my words as the memories flowed, and to my tech-savvy daughters Katharine and Stephanie, and my son, Keith, and his wife, Caroline, who coached me through the process of embedding photographs, managing page layouts, and shaping the book you now hold in your hand...

This eagle would never have landed without all of you.

CONTENTS

Love, Mrs. Euker

PROLOGUE

Happiness can be found in the darkest of times if one only remembers to turn on the light.

Albus Dumbledore

This book about teaching would never have been written if I hadn't been diagnosed with breast cancer in 2013.

There was no history of breast cancer in my family, and when the initial biopsy returned "positive," I was terrified. Although, overwhelmed at first, I learned that I had early stage triple negative aggressive cancer, but was relieved and blessed that the tumor was detected in a yearly mammogram. The recommended treatment was minimal: a lumpectomy with the removal of several lymph nodes, four months of chemotherapy, once a week with three weeks in-between, and ending with one month of daily radiation treatments. I trusted the surgeon and my oncologist as I embarked on this medical adventure.

One of my main fears was losing my hair as a result of the chemotherapy. I had read horror stories of women's hair shedding in their food, in the shower, on their pillows and everywhere else. I was worried about that, as well as about looking bald and funny—my head is not my best physical attribute.

Before that happened, I wanted my hair cut.

I invited my husband, children and grandchildren, and my lifelong friends to participate in a "Mimi Hair-Cutting Day" two weeks after my first treatments began. On a Sunday, we all gathered in my family room, and each person took a turn cutting off a piece of my hair, with the youngest grandchildren going first because they were the least afraid.

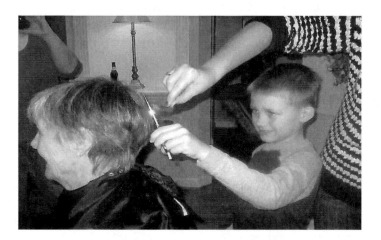

My grandson Ethan (age 8).

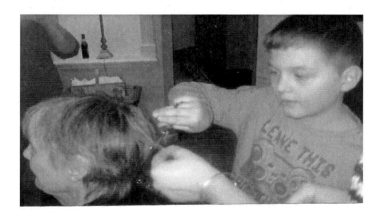

My grandson Carson (age 8).

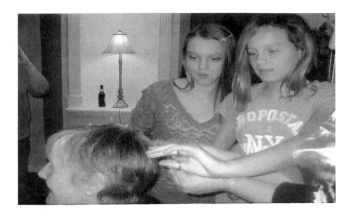

My granddaughters, Abby (age 11) and Hannah (age 12).

My daughters went next, then my friends, and finally my husband. Carl had the most difficult time, as he loved my long silky ponytail when we were in high school and college, my permed curls in the '90s and even my more recent gray bob.

But he resolutely took his turn.

After everybody finished, my two pre-teen granddaughters escorted me to the bathroom, where they applied colorful, but tasteful makeup to my ordinarily pale face, and delicately gelled and styled my remaining sprigs of hair. I then sashayed out to the waiting audience for my big "reveal." There was much clapping and hooting, and a few tears.

I looked beautiful.

My daughter Katharine celebrating with me.

Because the haircutting occurred two weeks before Christmas, once the scissors were put away and the floor covering with its delicate swirls of curls was shaken, folded and stored, we went into the kitchen to decorate Christmas cookies and enjoy a delicious potluck supper together.

I was so touched by my family's courage and love that afternoon that I wrote an essay about that day and created a book for Christmas with photos to give to each one who was there. My family and friends made me less fearful, more confident and stronger that day. As the rest of my hair gradually fell out, I was able to look at my bald head in the mirror.

And smile.

My journey through eight months of treatment prompted me to consider important issues. I wondered why I was put on earth and what I had contributed during my time here. My family had always been my purpose and my stability, but outside of my commitment to them, what had been my *raison d'être*? Seven decades is a long time to take up space on this planet, and I wanted to know that what I had done mattered.

So, I began thinking.

And then I began *writing*.

Although teaching had always been a most rewarding career, I began considering the *specifics* of the *why* and *how* I had spent those twenty years, and just what precisely had made the profession so compelling to me. As I sat on my sofa during that winter in front of the fireplace, watching the snow cover the garden, curled up in the warm, electric blanket that my sister had given me, and wearing the delightfully soft and decorative hats people had made for my bare head, I remembered.

Because of the chemotherapy treatments, I was having trouble eating and concentrating, but as I reflected on my years in front of the classroom and my relationships with my students, I was changed; I could focus more effectively, and my appetite even returned. During this contemplative time, I realized two things:

My students continued to impact me, even in my illness, and I had become a bit of a storyteller.

Many years ago, I read the 1964 bestseller *Up the Down Staircase*. In this honest, account of a public-school teacher's first year, Bel Kaufman described the joys and challenges of being in the classroom, and the absurdities of dealing with administrative decisions that she felt often interfered with students' learning. I remember laughing at her comical prose, but also being inspired by her words and example.

I have not read many "teachers' stories" since that time, and perhaps that is why I am so determined to write mine now. I do not consider myself a writer, so I began with some trepidation. However, as I put pen to paper, more and more of my teaching stories came back to me. The remembering summoned delight and pleasure, but it was the notion that capturing my thoughts and professional experiences might be a gift to my children and grandchildren that kept me going. I wanted them to come to know their Mimi, not only as a mother and grandmother, but as a teacher as well. As I re-read these accounts, I am filled with pride and gratitude.

Looking back, I realize that as with Sarah and Abraham of Old Testament fame, I followed my *calling,* and was rewarded beyond my deepest dreams. I found renewed gratitude for the opportunities I was given to see life more clearly, the time to appreciate that feeding one's soul with hope expands one's perspective, and the realization that the people I encountered during my teaching career changed me in ways I could not have imagined. Because of my experience with young people, unlike many of my generation who see the world in an unfavorable light, I envision the future with hope.

Through all of the ups and downs of teaching high school students, I learned much about tenacity, integrity, courage, humor (we laughed a *lot*), kindness, creativity and honor. The joys and successes as well as the exhaustion and disappointments of years in the classroom have made me a stronger and braver person. My students were my models.

Many years ago, when the darkness of my breast cancer diagnosis descended and my teaching memories surfaced, I began writing. As Albus Dumbledore inspired the pupils at Hogwarts to do in *Harry Potter*, I "turned the light on."

This memoir is the result of that light.

LOVE, MRS. EUKER

Growth is painful. Change is painful. But nothing is as painful as staying stuck somewhere you don't belong.

N. R. Narayana Murthy

My name is Susan Cunningham Euker, and for many years, I taught high school students at Hereford High School in Baltimore County, Maryland. At any point during my career, if you had asked, I would have said that I had the best job in the entire state of Maryland; I loved my school, my students and my subjects. One of the courses I taught was the state-mandated health course, which I lovingly referred to as "drugs, sex and rock and roll." What a joy it was to be with seventeen-year-olds each day and discuss how making wise choices in their lives was beneficial.

In my opinion, teaching high school is a privilege. It is an opportunity to think, laugh, cry and guide young men and women into a world that generally fears and misunderstands them, and discounts their abilities to make positive contributions. Truthfully, teaching teens can be a daunting task, but a challenge those, who are willing to love adolescents, undertake with energy, compassion, and resolve.

I wanted to be one of those people.

Jewel Adams was a harbinger for me. Many years ago, Jewel was a senior in high school outside of Gettysburg, Pennsylvania, and I was her student teacher. At the end of my student teaching semester, Jewel wrote a note to me. After commenting on my "dowdy" wardrobe and suggesting I bring a younger person clothes shopping with me, she complained that I assigned too much homework. "After all, Miss Cunningham, it is *health*!" I chuckled a bit at her critique of my fashion choices and her denigration of a subject for which I was unapologetically passionate and was encouraged by her. In the last line of her note, Jewel wrote: "Miss Cunningham, you have the potential to be a good teacher."

Over the years, during my teaching career, I thought a lot about what Jewel had advised and foretold, and that led me to think about my own schooling and three dedicated teachers who had had the greatest influence on me, each for a different reason.

MRS. MCCLAIN

Mrs. McClain was my second-grade teacher at Montebello Elementary School in Baltimore City. Each morning, my friends and I boarded the public bus on a busy street, and then halfway to school, transferred to a second bus at an even busier intersection in downtown Baltimore, *a seemingly dangerous trip now, but an ordinary journey back then*. We carried our fare, one nickel, in our little plastic change purses and as we stepped on the bus, we confidently deposited our coin with its satisfying clink into the fare box next to the driver.

One drizzly day, I had worn my brand new, *prized* red boots to the bus stop, and as I climbed the steps of the bus with confidence and a dash of brio, David, one of my schoolmates, made fun of my beautiful red sparkly, boots.

Everybody laughed.

After taking our seats on the bus, David snickered again and made another unkind comment.

That was just too much.

Nobody made fun of my red boots.

And so, naturally, I did what any independent, spirited, feisty seven-year-old girl would do. I hauled off and punched David right in the nose.

Blood spouted instantly from what appeared to be every orifice in his head, and I was scared to death.

When we arrived at school, Mrs. McClain met the bus as she always did, took one look at David and dispatched him to the school nurse. She sent *me* to the principal's office where my parents were eventually ushered in. I do not remember what was said, but I do know that I never hit anyone ever again.

Mrs. McClain made certain I faced the consequences.

I was embarrassed and humiliated, and I had to *apologize* to David. I reluctantly did what I was asked, but I did not mean one word of what I said. My fingers were crossed behind my back the entire time.

He deserved every bit of that punch.

Even so, I had learned an important life lesson. You can't solve your problems with fisticuffs.

And David? Well, he went on to become president of the student council at my high school, was an honor graduate of the United States Naval Academy in Annapolis, and as I write this, is most probably running a small country somewhere in the world.

I am quite certain that he would not remember what transpired that rainy day... but I do.

MR. RIEFNER

Carter Riefner was my high school CORE teacher. CORE was literature, social studies, spelling, composition, geography and pretty much everything we studied except math and science. So, I had Mr. Riefner for at least half of the school day.

And he was a *formidable* teacher.

Not only was he extremely knowledgeable about everything he taught, but he also made tedious historical subjects interesting and relevant to our lives. For example, to expose us to the beauty of the arts, Mr. Riefner had a *real* ballerina with her fluffy tutu and her pink satin ballet toe shoes come to class and demonstrate her craft. I had never been in the presence of such beauty before, and I loved it.

Is it dissatisfaction or contemplation shown on Mr. Reifner's face as he listens to a student's answer?

Mr. Riefner in the high school yearbook.

We read great works of literature, such as *Romeo and Juliet, Ivanhoe, Rime of the Ancient Mariner,* and discussed the poetry of Sir Walter Scott, Walt Whitman, and Edgar Allen Poe. As teenagers, we were truly inspired by the daily exposure to great writings. Moreover, Mr. Riefner was the first teacher I can remember who treated us as if we were pre-adults and were preparing for college. He loved to hear us discuss issues, and I loved to hear him teach.

I couldn't wait to see him each day.

Unfortunately, we were rarely exposed to women authors. This was more a statement of the times, than a lack of talented female writers. Women's issues were not a priority. Only now have we come to appreciate how severely limited our vision and horizons were. What a shame for the young women in our class, and the young men as well, to be deprived of the talents of overlooked women writers. In today's classrooms, students read works by Mary Shelley, Maya Angelou, Sandra Cisneros, Toni Morrison, Harper Lee, Alice Walker, Jeannette Walls, Zora Neale Hurston, and Lorraine Hansberry, as well as other acclaimed writers.

Despite my deep affection for Mr. Riefner, I had always been a rather indolent, disinterested student. I continued to do little to no homework, didn't study for tests, or really do anything academic in school. Even *he* could not change that. On more than one occasion, he had warned me that I was not doing well and that I had better start working or I would fail the class. In my know-it-all fourteen-year-old worldview, I did not believe Mr. Riefner *could* fail me because I was in a top section made up of college-bound students, and *everybody* had to pass.

Or, so I thought.

In homeroom at the end of the year as we were laughing and comparing our plans for the summer, I opened my report card and saw "E" where my CORE grade was entered. I had failed literature, social studies, spelling, composition, geography and most everything except math and science.

Stamped on the report card was:

This student will be passed on as 'will work.' Any grade lower than a "C" in the next marking period will result in the student repeating the grade.

I was in shock.

To better understand my plight, you need to know two things about me:

1. My mother was an honors graduate of the University of Oregon and was voted one of the eight best dates on campus her senior year. She had always been successful in nearly everything she did, and now her daughter had completely let her down. How could my mother have a firstborn child who was such a *failure? And, how could I face her?*

2. Ironically, at Mr. Riefner's urging, I had run for class office and won the election. I was the class vice president, and now technically, I was not *really* going to be in that class.

I could not believe it. How could the school do this to me? (I wasn't at the point yet where I understood that "*they*" did not do it. "I" had.) Stunned, I took my report card home fearing what my parents would say. All of my life, teachers and principals had told my parents I was not working up to my potential. "*They*" said I was a lazy student. B*ut this?*

To my parents' credit they did not say a word that afternoon. Their disappointment was palpable, but they knew this was my mess and that I would have to clean it up myself. Also, despite my feigned indifference, my mother instinctively knew how truly devastated I was over my failure, and she had confidence that I would make the changes I need to make.

And, I did.

A lot of soul-searching took place over that summer, and when school began that fall, I demonstrated some new behavior; I actually *did* my home-work and *studied* for tests. As the first report card period came to a close, I was terrified. If a student does not do well *because* she has not worked, it is always comfortable for her to say, "Well if I had worked harder"... I used that excuse a lot. But what happens if a student works really hard and she still does not do well? *What does that mean?*

I lifted the envelope flap of that November report card slowly, with shaking hands, buying into the old adage that the more gradually you open a report card, the better the grades are. The first letter grade I saw was for biology and I had earned an "A." I was incredulous. I had never had an "A" in my life, in anything. The other grades were "B's" and "C's," but I was so thrilled and relieved that I do not remember much else.

What I do recall is running to Mr. Riefner's room before I left for home that day with my report card in my hand and tiptoeing through the doorway as he was grading papers. With a quivering voice I asked Mr. Riefner to look at my report card. He took the card from my hands, studied it for a minute, looked at me with a knowing and confident smile, and said words that changed my life.

"Susan, I knew you could do it."

Every semester after that, I took my report card to Mr. Riefner before I showed it to my parents, and every semester his smile became brighter. He had been the teacher brave enough to fail an honors student because he knew she could do more. Mr. Riefner had simply refused to let my laziness and self-destructive tendencies determine my future.

At the end of that year, Mr. Riefner signed my yearbook with a reference to *The Taming of the Shrew*. "To Sue," he wrote," a Kate to be tamed."

He was my favorite teacher.

I continued studying and working hard, earned straight "A's" my senior year, was elected to the National Honor Society, and attended a highly competitive college where I graduated with honors in the department of education. I then spent most of my life teaching, so, if you consider it, I never really left the classroom.

After retiring from teaching, Mr. Riefner lived in a nearby retirement complex where I had the opportunity to visit him on three occasions. Once he even invited me to have lunch with him in the dining room where we talked about those days so many years ago and how I loved my teaching career as he had loved his. Each time I saw him, I reminded him of my story, and each time I told it, he smiled as he remembered.

Carter Riefner passed away shortly before his 100th birthday. I attended his funeral. All these years later, he remains my inspiration.

DR. SUSAN RADIUS

I met Dr. Susan Radius when I was thirty-eight years old and had entered graduate school to complete my master's degree, Baltimore County's requirement to re-enter teaching. Dr. Radius was a legend at Towson University, and those of us in the graduate program were more than a little in awe of her. But more intimidating to me was that she taught graduate level statistics and quantitative analysis. These were courses I was required to take ahead of writing my graduate thesis, and these were the courses that terrified me. The last math course I had taken had been in high school, and to say I squeaked by is a kind overstatement. I was not, and never had been strong in math.

As I began the first course Dr. Radius taught, I joined a study group made up of much younger women, who seemed savvier than I about what was going on in class. The group frequently studied together, and over the next three years, I came to value their patience and support as I wended my way through these difficult courses and required exams.

At the end of our regular coursework, we also studied for the five separate two-hour exams on every aspect of our graduate school health science curriculum, examinations we had to pass in order to receive our diplomas. With diligent work, group support, and lots of M&Ms, we all passed, which resulted in some well-deserved and grateful celebration.

Back row, left to right – Pat Heineman, Kathy Renzi,
Dr. Susan Radius, Maggie Ivusich.

Front row, left to right – Carol Kolb, me, Susan Eisenberg.

The most challenging part of graduate school is writing the thesis, a major paper involving a statistical analysis and conclusions on the topic the student has chosen. I opted to study a group of special needs students with whom I was working at the time. My paper analyzed the success of the program in which the students were enrolled. I worked for two years on the study and the paper, and because Dr. Radius was my thesis advisor, I met with her frequently.

Each time I brought my paper to her for editing, I left with so many red marks on the pages that I struggled at times to read what I had written. With Dr. Radius' encouragement, expertise and guidance, I eventually completed a surprisingly professional paper, defended my thesis orally before a panel of health science department professors, and handed it in. I could not have accomplished any of this work without her.

Although I didn't consider my schedule to be overwhelming at the time, in looking back I realize how important Dr. Radius' support and honesty were to my success and even to my survival. Over the years, our study group, including Dr. Radius, who I now call "Susan," meets several times a year for dinner, and as we re-connect, we appreciate how important we were to each other *then* and, interestingly, how important we are to each other *today*. We have all remained close friends.

Six years is a long time to be in graduate school. I was married, raising three children, and holding down two jobs, one as a graduate assistant at Towson University in the morning, and the other teaching at a local middle school in the afternoon. These posts helped pay my tuition.

As a result of these time demands, my family was forced to take more responsibility around our home, and that often added to the tension. Mom was simply not there to do all the things she had always done. My school-aged children managed to keep up with their homework, wash their own clothes, make their own lunches, keep their rooms reasonably clean, and generally assume more of the responsibility of caring for themselves than they had before.

At the time I felt I had lost contact with our day-to-day lives. I struggled to remember where my children were from time to time, and I hated it. My husband was particularly helpful in covering some of my usual duties and continuing to manage his responsibilities as well. In an attempt to stay connected, we scheduled family council meetings. Inspired by psychologist Alfred Adler, whose work I had discovered during my graduate studies, these mandatory meetings brought us all together, and guided us. By using *Robert's Rules of Order,* we managed to keep our family more organized and in sync with one another.

Each time we met, one of us was the president and led the meeting, while others took turns taking the minutes. We covered old business, new business, and devised ways to modify our routines to become more efficient. Everybody had a say. Duties rotated weekly, so even my youngest took a turn at leading our family discussions. I saved the minutes from those meetings in a folder, and thirty years later, we still re-read them, laugh, and remember that pressured, but life-changing time.

As I reflected on my student Jewel's original comments to me about the qualities of a "good teacher," Mrs. McClain, Mr. Riefner and Dr. Radius were the ones who taught me what a "good teacher" is. First, a "good teacher" is one who lets you know that fists are no way to settle differences. Second, a "good teacher" is one who helps you discover that you can do the thing you think you cannot do. Lastly, and most importantly, it is the "good teacher," who will not accept ordinary from you, and who is strong enough to force you to stretch beyond your boundaries even if you fight them all the way.

The stories in this memoir are dedicated to the many students during my years of teaching who encouraged me to strive to be a hard-working teacher, a devoted mother, a loving grandmother and most importantly, a "good" person unafraid to challenge the unknown. Becoming "unstuck" and moving to where I "belonged" was a compelling journey. Your support was indispensable.

Thank you.
Love, Mrs. Euker

REMEMBER WHY
YOU STARTED

Someday, you will look back and know exactly why it all had to happen.

Unknown

After I graduated from college, I taught middle school for five years, and then retired from the classroom to raise our three children. I was a stay-at-home Mom for ten years, and I loved every minute of my life. Returning to teaching was not something I was planning to do.

However, that changed.

When my children were in middle school and my husband and I saw college expenses looming, I decided to find gainful employment to help with our projected financial obligations. As I perused the newspaper's Help Wanted ads, I realized that there was not much for me to do. I discovered that companies do not hire people who excel at diaper-changing, floor-sweeping or carpooling, and to be perfectly honest, I had spent the last ten years of my life doing pretty much these tasks as well as other child-related activities. Although I loved being at home, it was now time to move on and contribute in the wider world. To do this, I had to leave the cocoon.

In a quest for summer employment I was hired to be a *Kelly Girl* as part of *Kelly Services*, the national temporary office-staffing agency. The only job I could get was stuffing envelopes for eight hours a day in a room with no radio, TV, windows or any other kind of stimulation. At the end of that first day, I left with a screaming headache and a vow to find something else out there that I could do. My extroverted, hyperactive personality was drowning in that sea of calm.

That evening, my husband and I discussed my desire to return to teaching. I had taught when we were newly married, however I had not been in the classroom for many years, and my state teaching certificate had expired. I wanted to look into graduate school to earn the credits I needed for re-certification, but I was terrified of taking the dreaded Graduate Record Exams. In spite of my misgivings, my husband encouraged me to go for it.

I had made a huge mistake in college by not taking the qualifying exams during my senior year. Now I feared I would not do well enough, especially in math, to qualify for admission. When I called Towson University and found out that the GREs were not required, I was ecstatic. I applied to the physical education master's program and was accepted for classes beginning that fall.

At the completion of twelve credit hours in physical education, I decided to change my field of study. Teaching middle school physical education no longer appealed to me. I thought I wanted to teach a more academic subject. I loved the physiology of the human body and I was interested in teaching older students about to enter the adult world.

After much research, I chose to major in health science administration. I thought if I ever wearied of high school that I could move into the business world. The new initiative in large corporations at that time was the hiring of health educators to offer in-house mental, physical and nutritional education and facilities to improve staff's wellness. For a time, I considered entering the field of corporate health. In the meantime, completion of high school health was a new requirement for graduation in Maryland, and I knew the state would be hiring more health teachers. This particular program at Towson University gave me several career options, and I was encouraged by the flexibility this degree would afford.

It took six years attending school part-time to achieve my goal of becoming a teacher, and when I graduated, I was offered two potential positions in the Baltimore County School System. The Health and Physical Education Supervisor called me on a Friday and said that I could teach eighth grade physical education in a newly opened middle school in Hereford with a well-known and beloved woman as my department chairperson, or I could go to Hereford High School to teach health part-time. The only catch was he could not guarantee the high school health position would be full-time the following year, but the part-time position was open now. He asked me to let him know which job I preferred by Monday morning.

I faced an unsettling weekend.

After weighing the options with my husband, I still could not decide which teaching position was better for me. On one hand, the eighth-grade physical education assignment was tempting because it was something I had done before. The department chair was much respected, and the school was only two years old and state-of-the-art. On the other hand, I had spent twelve semesters in graduate school preparing to teach health, and although the thought of being in high school in a regular classroom instead of the gym was a bit daunting, I felt I needed to use the education I had received.

My decision was made the following day.

I find that often in life we are given guidance from very surprising places, and that is what happened to me in this instance. On Sunday my family attended church, and because our pastor was on vacation, one of our friends preached the sermon. In his homily, Don reminded us about how in the Bible God had commanded Abraham and Sarah to leave their land and follow His word without looking back. As difficult as it was for them to do this, Abraham and Sarah followed what they were called to do, and their lives were richly rewarded.

I knew in that moment that I would venture into new territory and teach health at Hereford High. Perhaps the subject was a bit more difficult and challenging, and working with this new population would be more humbling, but at that point, I truly believed that I was *called* to work with high school students. Following in the footsteps of Sarah and Abraham, I did not look back.

My decision was made, and my dilemma was resolved.

On the first day of school that September as I entered Hereford High School for the first time, I felt the butterflies flitting around in my stomach as if I were seventeen again.

The sweet smell of anticipation of a new and exciting year filled the halls. As I crossed the school threshold that day, I remember noticing two things. First, most of the students were as tall as I was and I felt dwarfed as I wound my way to my classroom, and second, most of the students' cars in the parking lot were nicer and newer than mine.

I was ready to learn *why it all had to happen.*

LEARNING A LESSON

*The most important days in your life are the day you are born
and the day you find out why.*

Mark Twain

I am a teacher. I don't think I actually knew that until one spring semester
years ago, even though I had been in the classroom for quite some time.

Until I met seventeen-year-old TJ, I was an educator. Not that there
is anything wrong with being an educator, it is just different from being a
teacher. Being an educator suggests a stronger academic approach to the
classroom, aptitude test scores and quantifiable measures. Teaching, on the
other hand, involves *listening to the small voice in your heart that validates
children the world has dismissed.* It is sharing a part of yourself and in the
process receiving far more than you give.

TJ altered how I viewed my role as a teacher—big, blond, unkempt,
anti-social, quiet, forgotten TJ. He taught me much about what I value about
myself and how those values transfer to my students. This disinterested,
taciturn young man showed me what my profession is all about.

TJ sat in the very back of my classroom alone, isolated for one entire
semester and, in spite of my efforts, did nothing—no assignments, no tests,
no class work, no participation, demonstrating no interest in much of anything. And he failed—flat.

I was curious about this unusual young man, and after checking confidential records in the guidance office that I was authorized to read, I discovered information that made the pieces of TJ's puzzle fit. His father had died when he was in the seventh grade, and TJ had great difficulty getting along with his alcoholic mother throughout his teenage years. He had a brother who was intellectually and physically challenged, and it was suspected that both children might have been abused. At that time, educators were bound by law to report any abuse issues, but there was not enough evidence in this case, to contact authorities. TJ's mother was so verbally abusive to the school administrators that they had trouble dealing with TJ's truancy.

Living in such a dysfunctional family, TJ's low self-esteem became clearer and his frequent absences from school were understandable.

I hurt for him.

Because the successful completion of health in high school was a graduation requirement, and because for some reason TJ wanted to graduate, he returned in the spring semester of his senior year for one final try. I had my doubts.

So did everyone else.

The semester began with TJ's characteristic disinterest. But one day as the class tackled the concept of self-esteem, something changed. I had my students tape blank pieces of paper on their backs, and I gave them five minutes to circulate around the room, find five people they did not know particularly well, and write down on the sheet one positive thing they had noticed about that person without the students seeing the adjective they had written. Afterwards, we sat down and discussed anxieties and feelings about completing this exercise, and I asked them to remove the paper from their backs and read silently what the other students had written. I next asked students to write a paragraph describing themselves as others saw them, and how they felt about what they had read. TJ did as he was directed. I wondered why.

Several weeks later, TJ approached me after class and asked if he could present his "personality collage" to the class. I agreed, even though the collage assignment had been due more than a month before and all the other students had presented their projects on a day when TJ had been truant.

Frankly, I was curious, and I told TJ that we would be delighted to see his collage.

When TJ came to class the next day, he had his collage with him, prepared to explain it to the class. The other students had presented elaborate posters with pictures, words and mementos arranged artistically on various sizes and shapes of tag board.

TJ's collage consisted solely of three farming magazines connected to one another by a piece of baling rope. TJ explained that farming was his family's business and that the baling twine was what held his life together. At the bottom of the three magazines was taped the piece of paper TJ had worn the day of the self-esteem activity. Written on it were "kind, funny, pretty hair, a nice person and caring." I hung the collage in the front of the room for all to see.

Students' collages.

As TJ returned to his seat that day, he moved his chair *up close to the last row of students*. I fought back tears and continued the day's lesson.

Sensing the privilege of experiencing TJ's presence, perhaps for the first time, the class remained unusually quiet.

Mrs. Euker's collage.

For TJ, it was the beginning of a connection.

TJ did graduate that June. Not only did he pass my class, but he also somehow passed twelfth grade social studies, the bane of every graduating senior. During the graduation ceremony, I felt *the joy of that small voice in my heart* when TJ received his diploma. I remembered the gift he had given me and my fourth period class that semester, and I cried.

As he passed me in the recessional that night, with his robes flying, his mortarboard askew and his diploma held high in jubilant celebration, he smiled, reached out, shook my hand, and winked.

I knew then I was a teacher.

TJ had taught me.

PHONE CALLS

Life is ours to be spent, not to be saved.

D.H. Lawrence

I began the human sexuality unit by addressing puberty and asking students to write about what they remembered about their physical, emotional, psychological, and social changes during that unsettling time. We then discussed how those early years had impacted their perception of themselves and their peers. After that lesson, we delved into different types of relationships.

One of my favorite lessons was the one defining love, what it is and what it isn't, and what my students expected from their love relationships. After having students copy down the curriculum's definitions and discussing the three types of love, *Philos, Eros and Agape*, I asked them to write a paragraph about who they loved and why they loved that person.

We discussed some of their answers, and then I had students put away all papers, pencils and books, and sit quietly. After several minutes, I posed this question: "Why do we wait to tell people we love how important they are to us, and why don't we say 'I love you' more often?" I challenged the class to think of the last time they had told someone that they mattered to them. Finally, I held up my cell phone and asked, "If you had one phone call to make, who would you call and what would you say?"

Often students would sit and stare at me, since use of mobile phones during school hours was forbidden, and they had no idea what I was asking of them. *Could this be a trick?* I could hear them thinking. Usually, I would just stand there quietly for a few minutes and then repeat my question.

In this second segment of silence, using my mobile phone, I called my husband or one of my children and talked to them in front of the class, telling them that I really appreciated them and that I loved them. Afterwards, I held my phone up and asked, "Who's next?" By that point, most of my students had caught on and the bravest ones would raise their hands volunteering to make a call. The whole class would listen intently.

Without the speaker option on those early mobile phones, we could only hear what the students in class were saying. However, the drift of the conversations was easily understood.

JOAN:

"Mom, this is Joan. I am calling to tell you I love you."

Silence.

"Mom, I'm at school."

 Silence.

"No Mom, I'm not in the principal's office. No, Mom, I'm not in trouble!"

TOM:

"Dad, I'm calling to thank you for all you do for me and to tell you I love you."

After a short conversation, the class heard Tom say, "You're welcome, Dad."

Then Tom passed the phone to Richard, the boy sitting next to him, who followed Tom's lead and telephoned his own father.

"Hi Dad. Just called to say I love you."

Silence.

"It's your son, Dad... pause... Richard.

Silence.

"Oh. I'm sorry."

Richard ended the call, red-faced, admitting to the class that he had reached the wrong number. Richard and the whole class dissolved in laughter.

The next day, Tom came into class laughing even harder and told the class that his father had told him how much he had appreciated his son's call, but that after that call, his Dad had received a call from some other kid he did not know, named Richard, who also had told him he loved him.

Undoubtedly, Richard had hit the re-dial button and Tom's father had received two love calls that day.

While Richard and the class chuckled about the mistaken call, not all of the telephone outreach fared as well. A young girl named Mary called her father and left a message on his work phone telling him she loved him. She thought he would be thrilled to hear her voice when he listened to his messages. However, her father became so worried about Mary and the call that he went straight home, picked up Mary's mother and drove to school.

Fortunately, I intercepted the couple in the lobby, explained the reason for the call, and apologized for the misunderstanding. Because they assumed Mary was in trouble, had left school, or was emotionally distraught, they were extremely concerned. After we talked, they most graciously thanked me for letting them know that their daughter was OK. From then on, I made students explain to the caller at the outset that the phone calls were part of a health class activity and that they were being made from school.

And, I wrote a note to Mary and her family apologizing again for the misunderstanding.

ALICIA:

Alicia sat in the front of my health class, and when she placed her call, we heard another student's phone ring in the back of the room... her best friend's phone, of course. I let her talk even though students were not allowed to use cell phones in school. Teachers were the only ones authorized to have cell phones and all the calls thus far had been made from my phone. I do not recall exactly what the girls said, but I do remember that two of the football players' names were mentioned with smiles and brief giggles.

ANDY:

Andy told the class he was going to call his grandmother. I had asked students to keep their calls brief so others could have a turn, but when Andy had his grandmother on the phone telling her that he loved her and appreciated all she meant to the family, he could not get her off the phone. The class listened attentively to his side of what was a touching conversation between a grandson and his grandmother, especially since Andy was the quarterback on Hereford High School's state championship football team, and a visible and popular young man.

Andy was finally able to gently and politely tell his grandmother goodbye. When he hung up, the whole class applauded. Five minutes later, the assistant principal's voice was heard over the loudspeaker instructing me to send Andy to the office for a telephone call. Ten minutes later, Andy returned wearing a big grin on his face.

"Yep, it was my grandmother telling me how much she loved me."

Andy graduated from Hereford, played football at Rutgers University, became the long-ball snapper for the Tampa Bay Buccaneers in the National Football league, and eventually went on to play for the Chicago Bears.

And, I expect he still calls his grandmother.

BRUNO:

Bruno was a foreign exchange student from Germany, and with my permission, he called his cousin in Hamburg, Germany. That day, the class was privy to a funny and entertaining conversation between two good friends, an ocean apart, who had not seen each other for months. Because Bruno was speaking in German, we did not understand a single word, but the smile on his face spoke volumes. Bruno thanked me profusely for allowing him to make the call; it had meant so much to him.

What I did not know was, at that time, long distance phone calls on my mobile phone plan were extremely expensive. When my husband saw the phone bill that month, we had a *curious* conversation. Fortunately, he agreed it was well worth the price for such an important call.

Teachers often supplement their classes with private expenditures and extra special additions to their lessons. It's just what teachers do often without even thinking about the expense.

Academic content is certainly important, but when I encountered students years after they had graduated, they often told me they remembered the "love call" lesson and others that prompted them to contemplate life issues. My greatest pleasure came from those lessons that resonated with students on an emotional level, and generally, I found that those lessons were overlooked when county curricula was written.

Often, these lessons also required that I purchase extra props for emphasis. I never minded, because I know many teachers dig deep into their own pockets to enhance their lessons. Our passion for our students requires that of us.

Kudos to my husband and other understanding spouses who agree that life is "not meant to be saved," and appreciate the extras teachers give to their students.

SAM

If you are thinking what everyone else is thinking, you are contributing to the average.

Anonymous

My first years of teaching health to high school juniors and seniors tested everything I had learned in graduate school. The course on human sexuality was a large part of the health curriculum, and based on what I was hearing about students' decisions relating to their love lives, I believed that this unit was particularly crucial. Not only did I have to be knowledgeable about the academic information, but I also had to present my lessons in a way that teens could and would listen.

The last challenge proved to be the most difficult.

I had not taught the sexuality unit to sixteen-and seventeen-year-olds before, and I was in murky territory. I needed to figure out how to approach delicate subjects and help students understand that loving someone was not the same as having sex. I wanted them to consider not only the physical health aspects and consequences of sexuality, but also recognize the emotional and psychological components of a healthy relationship.

I knew that some of my students were in serious and life-altering situations and I wanted them to have the educational tools to make good decisions. The girls in particular struggled with what they wanted and did not want in a relationship. I worried about these young women the most.

When I began teaching the unit on sexuality, I first had students think back on their own experience of puberty. I was especially interested in their assessment of the emotional and social transitions they experienced during those years. I believed introspection was an effective way to prompt discussions about sensitive topics, so I had students make an entry in their writing journal each day. I collected the journals several times during the week to gauge how students were doing. That is how, as a relatively new teacher, I learned my most valuable lesson.

Teens are not likely to share their personal lives with a teacher, especially on the pages of a journal. Trust and transparency need to be developed over time.

Sam taught me that.

Sam was a good-looking junior, popular with teachers and peers alike, responsible, honest, and a dedicated student planning on attending college. He was also self-confident and quite willing to voice his opinion on most every topic we studied. When it came to submitting journal entries about puberty though, Sam rebelled.

In a private conversation, he told me he had no intention of answering my questions because his sexual behavior was his private business, and I had no right to delve into his personal life. He went on to say that he thought the entire sexuality unit was intrusive and he was not happy about discussing such topics as intercourse, pregnancy and sexually transmitted diseases. I surmised that the specific anatomical language and the lessons about the impact of sexual intercourse on girls were uncomfortable topics for him. I knew Sam had a steady girlfriend, and I suspected these discussions were hitting too close to home.

Sam told me he wasn't going to do any assignments he did not like, and he did not care about his grade. This last statement surprised me because I knew Sam was an honors student considering several competitive colleges. Grades were important to him. I thanked Sam for his honesty, and I told him to ignore any assignment that made him uncomfortable.

He left class that day and we did not speak about the matter again.

I proceeded with my *intrusive* teaching, but modified my questions, using Sam as my barometer. If he really resented the questions I asked, then I softened the assignment somewhat. I trusted Sam and was learning from his feedback. However, I knew I had to weigh the information the students needed to know against the specific content Sam did not like.

In all, I thought I had struck a good balance. By the end of the semester, Sam had completed enough work to earn a respectable "B" on his report card, and I calculated I had earned about the same for my teaching.

I learned what I needed to know about my students and their comfort levels, and I hoped Sam had learned something about human sexuality. My most important lesson was to accept where my students were in their sexual choices, not judge their purity, and learn from them by listening with an open mind. Having been raised in a fairly "Victorian" era, I had to consider that sexual decisions made by my students were theirs to make, and theirs alone. My job was to give them information so they could make as healthy and appropriate decisions as possible.

As was my habit, I wrote students a letter at the end of the semester expressing my gratitude for their work in class. As they filed out of my room that day, I high-fived each one and reminded them that their remaining high school years would be what they made it. I shared with them the advice my father gave my sisters and me:

"Love many, trust few, but always paddle your own canoe."

My students had heard that maxim so many times that semester that they knew the aphorism by heart. I hoped they would remember its meaning, especially the girls.

As I returned to my desk that day, I pondered the value of my impact on the students and wondered if they had learned what I had hoped they would. Then I sat at my desk and continued the never-ending task of grading papers.

The following week was the beginning of a new semester, and when I returned to my room after lunch, I was surprised to find a large arrangement of gorgeous blooms that nearly covered my desk and filled my room with a breathtaking aroma. The bouquet was filled with yellow roses, pink carnations, daisies and beautiful pink and blue hydrangeas.

The attached note read:

"Mrs. Euker, thank you. It has been educational."

Sam

That is the first and only time I have ever received flowers from a student, and I will always remember Sam.

I often wonder if that was his intent. Sam liked approval and by sending flowers, he knew that gesture would set him apart from other students. I also still wondered about his girlfriend and if that relationship was the cause of his discomfort. Was Sam simply embarrassed by the depth of the information we discussed. Or, perhaps he found the information he learned from the course useful or was regretful about his resistance and just wanted to thank me.

I will never know the answer.

As teachers, any impact we may have on our students is often a matter of conjecture. Sometime if we catch a glimpse into our pupils' lives, we might experience a brief moment of understanding. It is rare happenstance when a teacher learns from a student, sometime years after the fact, that what and how they taught made a difference in their student's life. More often than not, we never know. As the great theologian, C. S. Lewis wrote: "The task of the modern educator is not to cut down the jungle, but to irrigate the desert."

I learned much later that Sam's mother had been one of my young son's pre-school teachers, and I treasure one of the many ironies in life that during one pivotal semester, two mothers cared for the other's son.

I will always remember that too.

OPHELIA

I do not know how my story will end, but nowhere in my text will it ever read I gave up.

Unknown

In the 1990s I read *Reviving Ophelia: Saving the Lives of Adolescent Girls*, a book written by psychologist Mary Pipher, who contended that we lose our young girls spiritually and emotionally somewhere between elementary school and high school. She stated that girls begin to become subservient and are unable to stand up for themselves, and she used Ophelia from Shakespeare's *Hamlet* as an example.

Hamlet's girlfriend did everything he wanted. Apart from him, Ophelia had no identity. When Hamlet breaks up with her, and then murders her father, Ophelia, mad with grief, drowns herself. Ophelia believed she had no worth or value, and therefore, she had no future.

In her book, Dr. Pipher set forth ideas on how we can "revive" our young Ophelias and teach them to be assertive and self-confident during this formative period of their lives. She argued that young girls *could* learn to acknowledge their inner strength early their development and become strong enough to trust their instincts and stand alone when necessary. Dr. Pipher based her book on her experiences as a family counselor, and many of her suggestions came from families who successfully taught their young girls self-respect and leadership.

When I read this book, I was floored. I had taught young women for many years, and I realized I had no idea about the depth of their struggles. In the 1950s when I was a teenager, my girlfriends and I just played sports, studied, and did what we had to do to get by. I do not remember dealing with the self-doubt and waning confidence Dr. Pipher described. However, I readily acknowledge that my early life was lived in a simpler and safer era and I worried about how young girls were coping in the modern world.

At this time, my two daughters were in high school and my son attended middle school. As I thought about their lives and how they must be dealing with the trials of adolescence, I was struck by how much I did *not* know about the issues they were facing.

Even though I had completed my time-consuming graduate program, I still spent little time with them because I was establishing my career. I assumed they were fine. All three were hard-working students, had devoted friends and I thought they were happy and well adjusted. Reading Dr. Pipher's research was a revelation, and I made some critical changes. I prioritized one-on-one time with my children, trying to establish a more conversational relationship with them. I wanted to know how they were faring. What I discovered was troubling.

Ultimately, my two daughters began seeing an adolescent psychologist, at their request, and we transferred our son to a different school. His attitude was becoming concerning and he was acting out in school. His behavior towards his teachers was especially upsetting to me. What Dr. Piper had written affected me on a more personal level than I had anticipated, and my approach to mothering changed for the better because of her.

After much thought, I decided to organize an Ophelia Club at school for any girls who might be interested in personal development. Together I envisioned we would establish goals and plan activities that would enhance their growth, contributing to their maturation into strong, independent young women. I intended to target the girls in school who were so strongly attached to their boyfriends that they had little identity outside the relationship. I wanted these girls to learn that they had value and intelligence independent of their boyfriends. With Dr. Pipher as my guide, I hoped to help change lives.

With my principal's endorsement, I set the date for the initial meeting, put up signs in the school and had the proposed club mentioned in the morning announcements. My high school had four, ninety-minute classes with a one-hour break for students to eat lunch and participate in activities. This schedule worked perfectly for my Ophelia Club, as I was free that hour during the regular school day to hold meetings. Although I had no idea how many students would come, a few asked about the club, so I knew there was at least some interest.

On the morning of that first meeting, I was admittedly anxious for the activity period to begin. As the bell rang signaling the change of classes, I held my breath, waiting by the door to greet students.

I was astounded!

More than fifty students filed into my room to find out about this new organization, and to my surprise, many of them were boys. I couldn't believe it. Had my Ophelia Club struck a chord? Were there really that many students who were truly interested? I wondered what they expected and whether or not the club could meet their needs. Suddenly, the enormity of this club's potential dawned on me. *What an opportunity to help empower and inspire high school students.*

The bell rang sooner than expected, and I was elated by excited buzzing of the students as they left the room. Their laughter and happy banter were deeply gratifying to me. As teachers, we do not often see such hope and delight in our students.

That day, I did.

As the weeks went by, the Ophelia Club took shape. The students selected officers, brainstormed critical issues the group should address and wrote the organization's mission statement:

To encourage young women to confidently demonstrate leadership and to contribute to society in meaningful and significant ways.

Hereford Ophelia Club

17301 YORK ROAD
PARKTON, MD 21120

SEUKER@BCPS.ORG

dare to dream

Each week between thirty and fifty students participated in our activities. The pretzels, chips, veggies and other treats I brought continued to be a draw, and the students spent an hour once a week planning and discussing issues with which the teens were grappling. I was continually impressed by the students' leadership capabilities, self-direction and enthusiastic maturity in suggesting sensitive and controversial topics. One of their concerns was about male-female communication, especially when it came to "No means No." This was long before the #MeToo movement, and looking back, I realize that even then females struggled to be heard.

Boys continued to be involved, and their participation was an enriching part of our club dynamic. Initially, I speculated the boys came because the girls were there, but I soon learned that these young men were as interested in learning more about teen issues as the girls were, particularly relating to their romantic relationships.

Soon, the Ophelia Club was organizing student forums addressing male/female relationships, staging discussions about teen life and engaging parents on "back-to-school" nights, demonstrating their support of faculty by beautifying staff-only lavatories and teacher workrooms with new paint, wallpaper, fresh flowers and providing anonymous treats and thank you notes for teachers and other support personnel.

Ophelia Club members reached out to other groups, initially to the eighth-grade girls at a sister middle school. Soon club members were invited to speak at a local Lions Club meeting, and later shared our school's Ophelia Club experience with other middle and high schools in Maryland.

For several years, the male students continued to attend, and one year a boy was elected Ophelia Club president. The annual male/female question and answer forum was especially popular with both sexes, and I was told again and again how students appreciated the honesty and insights these sessions provided. Truthfully, the boys offered a perspective that I do not believe the girls had considered, particularly when we discussed feelings and viewpoints about the opposite sex. Even *I* gleaned some formation that helped me better understand my son. Eventually, the boys' attendance dwindled, but while they participated, their contributions were fun and enriching.

As club members became more self-confident, they began speaking to professional organizations. The group's first major presentation was in downtown Baltimore at the Maryland State Governor's Council on Adolescent Pregnancy Conference.

Ophelia Club members leading a forum.

Hereford High School's Ophelia Club attended that conference for the next few years as well as the Maryland State Guidance Counselor and Home and Hospital Teachers Conference and other local conventions.

Ophelia Club members were eager to share the teen experience with anyone who wanted to listen.

I watched young people who had been afraid to speak in public present their talks clearly and confidently. Some students, who had been hurt or damaged by past decisions, were willing and quite capable of sharing their newly acquired wisdom. Their eye-opening accounts guaranteed that the audience was learning a lot more about teenage life than they might have expected. The presentations emphasized courage and hope. Often, when the students spoke, I was moved to tears.

*Ophelia Club presenting at a guidance conference in
downtown Baltimore, Maryland.*

Our school's Ophelia Club members also traveled outside Maryland. The year before I retired from Hereford High School, some of the Ophelia Club members flew to Hartford, Connecticut to address the annual meeting of the American Alliance for Health Physical Education, Recreation and Dance, a national organization of more than twenty thousand professionals dedicated to advancing the field of physical fitness.

When I announced that our club had been selected, the girls screamed with delight. The initial celebrating, however, was followed by a brief period of self-questioning and uncertainty when the girls considered what was ahead of them. When I reminded them of their goals and the club's mission statement, they settled in and began planning their presentation.

Ophelia Club officers planning for Hartford.

For months, the seventeen girls who were going to the conference rehearsed what they wanted to say and do, clarified what my role would be, designed and printed T-shirts to wear advertising "Hereford Ophelia Club" on the front and "Dare to Dream" on the back.

When I was given my own personal T-shirt to match the girls, I was overwhelmed with emotion. I remember wishing I were sixteen again and a Hereford High School Ophelia girl. The girls were so proud of their accomplishments. I knew I was observing the opening of a cocoon, seeing my once hesitant girls morph into fearless, confident young women. The transformation from timid girls to dynamic enthusiastic advocates for them-selves as well as for other young women was awe-inspiring. I was privileged to witness the emergence of these beautiful butterflies.

My granddaughter, Abigail
wearing my Ophelia Club T-shirt.

As the day of departure approached, all of our plans came together. We boarded the plane and the captain made us feel even more special by announcing our group's name and where we were going, although the girls were hard to miss in their florescent pink T-shirts. Everyone in the cabin clapped.

After a short flight to Hartford, we arrived safely at our hotel. Many of the girls had not experienced the grandeur of a sophisticated hotel lobby before, the imposing bank of elevators, or the spacious accommodations. The girls oohed and aahed over our elegant surroundings and the hotel staff's lavish attention. In time the girls' excitement devolved into exhaustion, and finally lights out.

After breakfast, where the girls alternately ate everything or nothing, depending upon the number of butterflies in their stomach, we marched into the hotel's ballroom where more than one thousand educators had assembled. We listened to the keynote speaker, and then wound our way to the room designated for our breakout session. More than one hundred educators filed in to hear our Ophelia Club presentation.

Once I explained the focus of the club and the reasons for its creation, I invited the girls to come forward. One at a time, each of the girls introduced herself, identified the many activities in which she was involved, and other positive information about herself.

The girls then orchestrated an activity called "Corners" in which a question or statement relating to teenage girls was read, and the audience was instructed to indicate their level of agreement with the statement by walking to the labeled corner of the room that most reflected what they believed about what had been stated. The corners were labeled: agree somewhat; agree completely; disagree somewhat or disagree completely.

Some of the professionals were startled by the statements the girls shared including statistics that show twenty-five percent of teenage girls report being drunk during their first sexual experience; that marijuana is the drug of choice among most sixteen-year-olds; and that fifty percent of students questioned said their parents had no idea where they went for parties.

The groups discussed each topic in their respective corners for five minutes, and then the Ophelia girls shared the statistics and research supporting each statement. Many of the participants had no awareness of the widespread sexual activity and alcohol consumption of teens. They were especially surprised and concerned by the statistic that showed most parents did not know where their teens were when they went out at night. Several in the audience challenged what the girls were reporting, arguing that this was not a phenomenon of which they were aware. The majority of attendees, however, were shocked.

Once everyone returned to their seats, I commented on how difficult it is to be a teenage girl based on the statements we had just heard and noted how little adults really know about what young girls experience on a daily basis. I *re-introduced* the Ophelia girls, and *this* time each girl took the microphone and told what was *really* going on in her life—depression, divorce, parents losing jobs, ill siblings, acute injuries that prevented them from playing the sport they loved, drug and alcohol addiction, college rejections, family secrets, and more.

Although I was aware of some of the challenges these girls were facing, what they revealed that day stunned me, and I sat in the back of the room heartbroken that so much of their lives was hidden, even from me. I felt tears on my cheeks. Not wanting to divert the attention from the girls, I dabbed at my eyes with a clumsily found tissue.

While I knew most of the girls' parents, I had not a clue about the turmoil at home. I had given the girls a lot of leeway in what they were to say at the conference, and they took advantage of the opportunity to demonstrate the leadership and courage for which we continually strived. For me, this was an overwhelming and honest insight into my Ophelia girls' lives, and I was so proud of their openness and vulnerability.

I was reminded once again of what Dr. Pipher had written; most of us see young girls in a superficial light, and often we have little concept of what is really happening in their young lives. That day, my Ophelia girls' message was truthfully and bravely presented. These highly successful student leaders had issues that no one suspected, and in spite of their challenges, they were somehow able to succeed in both their academic and social lives. When I contemplated how they were able to flourish when so many other young girls in similar circumstances were not, I remembered what Dr. Pipher had written and I began to understand.

At the conclusion of our presentation, the girls explained how the Ophelia Club had provided a safe place for them to meet, where they could receive honest, caring support, and how the club had allowed them to reach out to others in the community. They talked about a "sisterhood," and how they had supported one another along their high school journey in healthy and confident ways. It was at that point I realized that Dr. Pipher's insights and guidance had made a world of difference to my students. Their lives were better because of her.

Several months after this conference, I had the opportunity to hear Dr. Pipher lecture at a local college. Following her presentation, I was able to tell her what her book had meant to my girls. After a smile and thank you, she gave me a hug.

When I retired from teaching, a friend of mine mentored the club that continued to be involved in the community by speaking to professional groups about teen life. The year after my retirement, I was touched when the girls asked me to accompany them to a conference in Providence, Rhode Island. I was introduced as the club's founder and asked to recount my initial vision for the club and what I saw as its significance. I spoke with honesty and much pride, and I am thrilled that the seed planted by Dr. Pipher so many years ago still survives.

After graduation, many of the Ophelia girls made their mark in the community. Some attended prestigious universities and colleges and earned master's degrees and beyond. One girl, struggling with anxiety and depression and was "cutting herself" in high school, later pursued a doctorate in psychology intent on helping teens who are depressed or addicted to substances.

Another girl, Kate, graduated from Goucher College Magna Cum Laude and Phi Beta Kappa with a degree in psychology, earned her Master's Plus degree, and co-authored a handbook on policies and procedures relating to students with special needs entitled *A Call to Inclusion,* which is used in every elementary and middle school in the Baltimore Archdiocese. She then served as a school counselor in two Catholic schools. Her younger sister, also an Ophelia girl, earned her doctorate from Stanford University after battling years of depression, and is presently a professor in the business school at Dartmouth University.

A fourth girl attended Duke University, aspiring to study medicine, but during her junior year while traveling to Africa to help design health programs for women in small, underdeveloped countries, she changed her direction. In a letter she described her work as "so Ophelia-ish." Armed with a master's degree in social work, she became a force for good in assisting struggling women in inner city environments.

Three of my Ophelia girls were close friends, and for an honors senior English project, costumed and filmed a documentary recounting the Shakespearean story of *Ophelia*. They proudly presented a DVD of their dramatization to me when they graduated, and it is one of my prized possessions.

During her first year in high school, another Ophelia girl tore her ACL so badly that she had to stop playing lacrosse, a sport she loved, and in which she excelled. Although devastated by the injury, instead of dropping the sport altogether, she spent time, with her father, coaching girl's lacrosse in the local recreation program.

Math and computers were her passion, and after graduating from Georgetown and Columbia Universities, she spends her volunteer time teaching young high school girls the latest in computer technology.

Another example of the impact of the Ophelia Club is Andrea, who was rather quiet and withdrawn during her first years in high school. She related to me that during that time, the only place she felt accepted was with the Ophelia Club. Supported and encouraged by the other girls, she began attending meetings, and although she did not serve as an officer, she was an active and spirited member. One of Andrea's favorite remembrances is of a light rail trip the club took to the Ronald McDonald House in downtown Baltimore to visit families dealing with life-threatening illnesses.

In college, this Ophelia Club member studied special education, graduated, and taught autistic children. Eventually, she married her high school sweetheart, Greg, and they have fostered four young siblings, ranging in age from ten months to seven years with plans to adopt. When they learned that the biological mother of the foster children was once again pregnant, they asked to care for that child as well. Within one year, this couple went from having a quiet house to raising five siblings in a warm, loving home.

Greg and Andrea's Family.

I was privileged to witness the adoption of all five children after two years of legal entanglements, prayers, and dedication on the part of the parents, their family and faithful friends. Many of the over one hundred witnesses in the courtroom to celebrate the adoption that day wore superhero clothing to honor the children's new family.

Andrea named her youngest daughter Riley Ophelia.

Another Ophelia girl is serving as a missionary in Russia with her husband and children. And there are so many more.

Looking back on my years with my Ophelia Club, I can now see how blessed I was to witness these young women as they formulated ideas and dreamed about what life *could* be. Expressing concern for others, sharing visions, developing gratitude and overcoming sadness and obstacles are the strengths they discovered together. I am a tougher, kinder, more introspective woman because of my girls.

Sparked by a book about teenage girls, I imagined a club where young women could come together and talk freely about their fears, hindrances and goals. It is amazing to me after all these years how the words of one woman could ignite a dream that would enable my Ophelia girls to become stronger, kinder, more self-confident women.

Books have the power to change lives and "me and my girls" will be ever grateful to Dr. Pipher for her pioneering research that drew attention to the plight of young girls and provided transformative guidance to revive Ophelias at Hereford High and elsewhere.

Thank you, Dr. Pipher.

Yearly Ophelia mentor luncheon where girls honored significant people in their lives.

Love, Mrs. Euker

Halloween shenanigans.

NEWS

Ophelia club conquers Connecticut

Meghan Roth

Ophelia, a prominent extra-curricular Hereford High is an organization designed for students to discuss topics surrounding women's issues and what it is like to be a teenager in today's society. Based on Dr. Mary Pipher's book, Reviving Ophelia, the club encourages its 10th, 11th and 12th grade members to reach their full potential and contribute to the world in a positive way. Mrs. Susan Euker, the "Oprah of Hereford High School", initially sponsored the club eleven years ago.

Recently the group of young girls traveled to Hartford, Connecticut to speak at the Eastern District Association Conference of the American Alliance of Health, Physical Education, Recreation and Dance about how the Ophelia Club has had a positive influence on their lives. Once there, each girl courageously addressed a significant conflict she faces and how participating in the Ophelia Club has helped her grow. The club members all sported pink t-shirts that read, "Dare to Dream" to express the hopeful and promising words that would encourage whomever to reach for the stars.

Aside from speaking at conferences, this philanthropic organization also participates in several community activities. The girls make Christmas care-packages for children in other countries and have parties for Mt. Washing-

Students in the Ophelia club pose in their pink t-shirts in the Conference hall in Connecticut. Here the group spoke out against difficult issues faced by today's females.

ton Children's Hospital and the Ronald McDonald House.

It is apparent that the Ophelia Club makes countless efforts to play a positive role in today's society. Mrs. Euker praises them saying, "I am continually blown away by these girls."

TUCKER

The greatness in life is to plant a tree in whose shade you will never rest.

Nelson Henderson

Tucker was not what anyone would consider an engaged student. The only thing I remember about Tucker is that he had been in a motor cross accident in ninth grade, and as a result, had become addicted to painkillers. I saw no evidence of his drug use when he was a student in my class, but I knew that he was struggling. After he graduated, I did not hear anything more about him.

Several years later, I served as one of our adult church leaders accompanying our youth group to shelters where they worked serving others. One of the places we visited regularly was a shelter for homeless men in downtown Baltimore, where we served meals and interacted with the residents.

The men who lived there were addicted to substances, and as a result, had committed crimes to fund their habit. Their rehabilitation plan was to stay drug-free and help run the shelter. In return, the shelter provided necessary skills, training and contacts to help the men find employment and return to their communities. Generally, the men were allowed six months to assimilate back into society. The "tough love" approach set strict rules and offered guidance to help the men succeed.

I thought it was a very hopeful program.

One Sunday night our youth group went to the shelter to serve a spaghetti dinner. After we set up the meal, we greeted about twenty-five men as they meandered into the dining area. As I observed, I noticed that many were older men who were dealing with aging issues as well as their addiction.

Midway along the dinner line, a young man, no older than twenty, was serving himself. I was curious, and although I could not see his face at first, as he turned toward me, I was astounded to see my former student, Tucker. He recognized me immediately, smiled, and came right over to greet me. He asked if he could sit with me, and for the next forty minutes Tucker told me about his life after high school.

Tucker's addiction to heroin, which had begun with his initial dependence on painkillers, increased to the point that he was "copping" drugs in the alleys of South Baltimore. He told me his parents had finally kicked him out of the house after he had repeatedly stolen from them as well as from his sister. As a result, he lived in his car on the streets of Baltimore.

Tucker said he had finally sold his car for drug money and was barely able to exist. Tearfully, he talked about four friends who died in his arms from heroin overdoses. Fortunately, Tucker had found his way to the men's shelter and was working on staying clean and completing his program.

As he spoke, I was quiet and feeling sad for this young man who had once been a student of mine. I remembered his smile, his quirky sense of humor and his purple Mohawk hairstyle. He was so different from the "usual" academic students at Hereford, but I had continued to trust he would be able to find his way after high school. His struggles were evident to me, and I was frustrated that I could do so little for him. I wondered what the school might have done differently to help prevent him from ending up where he was now.

We finished our dinner together, and I promised Tucker I would stay in touch. Only a month away from completing the program, he asked if he could visit me at school when he returned home. I told him I would be delighted to see him. We parted with a friendly hug.

Several months later, Tucker contacted me at school, and at my suggestion, we scheduled class time for him to speak to our high schoolers about his experiences. With my principal's permission, Tucker shared his life's story with my health classes. He was honest and upfront with my students about how his drug use had almost destroyed him.

My students were mesmerized.

I thought Tucker did a professional and complete job when he spoke, and my students loved him. Tucker spoke often to my health classes during the next school year. Coincidentally, *The Baltimore Sun* ran a lengthy article about teen drug use, and Tucker's family was featured. Photographs accompanied the interview, describing how he and his family had dealt with Tucker's addiction.

Tucker's life at that point projected health, hope and healing and I was so happy for him.

Months later when I stopped hearing from Tucker, I was concerned that things were not going well. I later found that Tucker was back on the streets using again, that he had been arrested for possession of heroin, and was in jail. I was devastated by the news. I had such high expectations for him. I did not hear any more from or about Tucker for quite a while, and I was worried.

Eventually, as Tucker was awaiting his court hearing, he sent a note asking me to write a letter of recommendation to the probation judge on his behalf. In the letter I explained how Tucker had spoken to my classes about addiction and expressed my belief that Tucker had potential if given another chance. I signed the letter and sent it off. I prayed that my endorsement would make a difference, but I was doubtful. To my happy surprise, I received a note from Tucker reporting his probation had been granted.

While out on bail, Tucker came to school to thank me in person. That afternoon, we discussed the possibility of his speaking to the faculty about what teachers could do to help students who were suspected of developing drug and alcohol dependencies in high school. Tucker believed that recognizing and referring troubled students early were crucial interventions, and he thought that teachers might benefit from hearing his story. My principal agreed that as soon as Tucker's ankle bracelet was removed, we could set up a meeting with the staff. Tucker and I were both excited and hopeful.

When the meeting date arrived, Tucker never showed up, and I didn't hear from him or run into him. Rumors reached me that he had returned to the streets and had been arrested yet again.

Eventually, Tucker wrote me from prison to ask if my students could correspond with him. For legal reasons, my principal forbade that contact, but said I could write if I wanted to. After much thought, I decided not to communicate with him because I felt that I had enabled Tucker enough, and that he would have to continue his journey by himself.

Years later, I learned from people who knew his family that Tucker had been killed in a motorcycle accident on his way home from the beach.

He had been clean and sober for five years.

Because Tucker had overcome so many difficulties and remained drug-free for so many years, losing him was especially painful for all who knew and loved him.

After Tucker's funeral, I wrote to his mother and father expressing how much he had meant to me and to the young people in my health classes, and I attached a preliminary copy of this essay. I told them I was beginning to chronicle my teaching memoirs and that Tucker's story had been one of the first stories I had written. I shared that Tucker had remained in contact with me during his relapses and had allowed me to better understand him. I expressed my gratitude at having had that opportunity because Tucker taught my students and me so much about decision-making, surviving hellish times and having the will to continue when the situation was grim.

I wanted Tucker's parents to know their son had mattered to me and to my students.

Rest in peace, Tucker

The tree you planted stands tall.

COACHING

Character, my friends, is a byproduct. It is produced in the great manufacture of daily duty.

Woodrow Wilson

A t most high schools, one of a teacher's additional responsibilities is to sponsor an activity or coach one of the high school sports teams. Hereford High School had a strong athletic program, and over the years, fielded many competitive teams. What the school did not have, however, was a badminton team, and several Baltimore County schools were interested in starting a badminton program.

The following year, my principal asked if I would be willing to coach badminton as there were more than thirty students who wanted to play. He enticed me by saying that one student was a very strong player and had promised to be the primary student-coach if there were a teacher-coach to handle the administrative work that came along with the assignment. I agreed even though I was already sponsoring the school's S.A.D.D. (Students Against Destructive Decisions) Chapter and had just recently begun the Ophelia Club, a young women's leadership program.

I went home that summer looking forward to meeting this young player who knew so much about badminton and who wanted to develop a team.

When I returned in the fall, I was dismayed to learn that the student so eager to coach the badminton team had moved to New York and that I was alone in my coaching commitment. I had no idea where to begin. I knew the basic rules of badminton from playing as a kid in our back yard, but coaching skilled players was a very different proposition.

As the season began, I was surprised and delighted (and a bit overwhelmed) to find forty students interested in "trying out" for the team. Of course, there would be no "trying out" as everyone who attended practice faithfully would make the team.

Although only eighteen players could participate in any individual competition, once the official matches were complete, the other players could challenge the opposing team in exhibition matches. This way, although no points were scored for either school, all players were able to participate. These matches also allowed the exhibition players to hone their skills, because during our weekly practices, we set aside one day where any player could challenge any other player to a match, with the winner moving into a first team slot.

Our badminton team was remarkably skilled. Some of the more experienced students taught their teammates the tricks of strong playing, and all of the players demonstrated outstanding sportsmanship. In fact, for eight of the ten years I coached, Hereford High School was voted the "Sportsmanship Award" by the other teams in the league. I took as much pride in that single recognition as I did in all of the collective and individual championships our team won.

One of the thoughtful things our players did at the end of each home match was to give the visiting team homemade snacks to eat on their bus ride home, a courtesy that made Hereford popular with our team's opponents.

2000 Varsity Badminton Team with coaches,
Mrs. McGarvey and me.

It is important to understand that badminton is a game where the two teams on the court call their own plays. If the shuttlecock lands in or out of the court, if it hits the net, or if a player accidentally hits the feathered projectile twice, it is the player's responsibility to make the fair call. Although this may be difficult to imagine in light of popular umpired sports, on most occasions, the correct calls were made. If a problem occurred, a team could request a coach to stand near the court to help with subsequent plays. However, this rarely happened.

Mark and Jeff were the men's doubles champions. They had won the men's doubles individual silver medal at the county championships the previous year and were favored to win the gold medal for a second year. The two were highly skilled athletes and were good friends off the court as well. Our entire team anticipated the end-of-the-year championships, where it was expected we would win the school's first-ever individual gold medal.

During one of the most competitive matches of the season, Mark and Jeff were in a game with an accomplished opposing team. Halfway through the third and deciding game of this particular match, the birdie flew over

Mark's head. He turned to watch it land, confident it would fall outside the line, awarding the point to him. However, as I watched the shuttlecock fly across the court, I saw it land just on the outside edge of the line, thus making it fair. I waited to see what Mark would do. From most angles, it was difficult to see the position of the birdie, but *I* saw it and I knew *Mark* saw it too. Other people were blocked from the view, so it was Mark's call.

As I watched Mark point inside the line, designating that it was fair and thus the opponents' point, I teared up. That single call cost Hereford's men's doubles' team the game but spoke volumes about the character of my player. Later, as I recounted to Mark's father what I had seen, he was filled with admiration for his son. Once again, I beamed with pride at the remarkable honor my team continually displayed. Mark and Jeff ultimately went on to win the silver medal at the individual county championships that year and the gold medal in their senior year.

Mark (left) and Jeff (right) proudly displaying their gold medals.

During the first several years I coached badminton, a healthy rivalry developed between some of the players on Hereford's championship football team and our badminton players. The athletes bantered back and forth, each singing the praises of their team and its importance to the reputation of the school; who were better sportsmen and who had more wins?

One afternoon after practices were over, *our* team challenged *their* team to a friendly badminton competition. Of course, the football team jumped right on that. What occurred that day was a sight to witness.

I watched high school students in a testosterone-laced gym serve, slam and drop-shot the birdie, bragging and laughing as they competed against each other. It quickly became evident that muscular strength was a detriment on the badminton court; the football players missed the birdie or frequently sent it flying out of the court. Some of the girls on the team joined in and were able to outplay the guys. At the end of play, there was a lot of handshaking and promises from the football players that next year's competition would end differently.

Of course, it never did.

As I look back on my days as a coach, I remember the triumphs all my athletes achieved and the championships they won for Hereford High School. I bask in the glory and recognition the team brought to our school, and I continue to delight in the last-minute, one-point victories the Hereford team won time and time again. But, more than all of that, I remember the integrity of my players.

I also remember Joe, who tried out for the badminton team as a ninth grader. On the first day of practice, I noticed that he was different from the other students. He pretty much stayed to himself. He was reluctant to interact with the other players, and I was a bit concerned about his ability to bond with the team.

Character development, kindness and fairness and learning to trust others in their growth, is in my opinion, more significant to students than most other lessons they learn. I call this "heart smarts." Our team not only encouraged and supported each other as players on the court, but they also genuinely liked being together. I wanted Joe to be a part of that equation.

That first fall season, I was elated to see Joe's gradual intermingling with the other team members. The team blended nicely, and the players encouraged Joe as he worked his way up to the second seed in mixed doubles a *highly coveted ranking.* Joe was an excellent athlete, threw himself into practice and as an upperclassman, went on to help the team clinch several team championships as well as winning the bronze medal in mixed doubles with his partner, Emily.

In October, several days before homecoming weekend Joe's freshman year, I noticed that my captains, George and Mary, were organizing the players to go out to dinner together that Friday and then afterwards to the homecoming dance. I was pleased to see that Joe joined them. The following week in practice, I learned that the team enjoyed their time together. For the next four years, I watched the team coalesce, continuing to nourish strong friendships.

When Joe graduated from Hereford, with honors, I was thrilled to be invited to his graduation party. At the gathering, Joe's mother asked to speak to me. After we found some privacy, she tearfully told me that Joe's performance on the badminton team had been the most significant accomplishment of his life. She went on to say that Joe had rarely socialized with others until the badminton players included him in the homecoming activities his freshman year. That single act of kindness, she continued, changed how Joe saw himself, and his proudest accomplishments were the badminton medals he had won.

In his senior English class, Joe wrote an essay sharing the effects joining the team had on him. It is one of the most open and vulnerable high school tributes I have read.

With Joe's permission, I have included part of what he wrote on the following page.

As Joe's mother talked that day, I was once again grateful that I had been given the privilege of working with such a remarkable group of young people. During my ten years as a coach, that pride and affection I felt for my players never waned.

The *byproduct of their character* continues to inspire me.

Badminton Forever
Joseph Gradowski

Badminton remains, now and forever, the happiest time of my natural life. For four years, behind everything I was striving for as a person, this activity was my sole engine for success. The passion, the friendship, the honesty, the love... It is living proof that there is heaven on Earth... and I have been there.

Four years ago, I arrived at the tryouts, a lowly outsider without a single teenage friend in all of Baltimore. I remember all kinds of thoughts racing through my head when they told me I was to be accepted. How could anyone have accepted someone like me? Me? A teenager too cowardly to strike up a conversation with even the most social person half his age?

Imagine my shock a year later, when I would realize I had not just been inducted into the official athletic sport; I had been accepted, no questions asked, into a family that would change my life forever.

If it weren't for those... *people*... I just don't think I would've lived through high school. They were the complete opposite of what I was expecting from athletes. I remember Mary. She was the first true friend I ever made anywhere. She would constantly walk over to me and... harass me into saying anything, for no reason. I was just so charmed to be able to chat with her and compete with her on the courts.

I had the most powerful smashes of anyone on the courts; and my coach, Mrs. Euker, possibly the most carefree soul I've ever known, utilized it very early on. "Joey," she'd say, "I want you to smash that birdie every time or I'll chop your ears off." That phrase became a running gag between us for two years... before she retired as our coach.

I was almost crushed at the end of my second year. Most of the team, my comrades, was graduating that year. George Mathews, the very man who first talked me into badminton, was leaving. Mrs. Euker, my truest mentor and friend, was retiring. Mary... *Mary*...

The weeks leading up to graduation I spent outside, desperate to avoid the subject with a long jog.

I was in the school band at the graduation. When the time came and the principal began to read off the names of the seniors, I hid my face and sobbed. I looked up for only a moment to see my friends receive their diplomas. When it was Mary's turn to go up, how I resisted screaming, I do not know. "She won't remember me," I thought, over and over again.

Just before her name was called, Mary looked over to the band and smiled at the badminton team members who were in the band... and smiled at me. I was stunned. She remembered me? In the midst of the largest moment of her life, she spared a thought for me?

Again, I say to you, moments like that and triumph like that... and *family* like that, you don't find here on Earth... but I have.

RYAN

The dictionary is the only place where success comes before work.

Vince Lombardi

I have learned that teachers cannot reach every student every time. Sometimes trying to do the right thing for the student backfires, and parents' involvement interferes in their learning process. Sadly, this is a lesson Ryan taught me.

Ryan was an average student, a nice-looking young man who was popular with students and was an enthusiastic participant in student activities. I taught Ryan eleventh grade English and enjoyed having him in class. He was *punctual* and *polite* (two of the *requirements* in my classroom), and he contributed to class discussions. Overall, I found Ryan to be a responsible and agreeable student.

The eleventh grade English curriculum involved reading great works, such as *A Raisin in the Sun, The Crucible, The Catcher in the Rye, To Kill a Mockingbird, a*s well as a selection of poetic and contemporary pieces. The intent of the course was to inspire students to examine their own lives and think about struggles other people have overcome while making decisions that contribute to the development of integrity, courage, and character.

The final assignment of the year was a five-hundred-word composition students had to write themselves. They were asked to formulate a thesis statement, research the body of the paper, and craft a final paragraph that included their findings relative to the original thesis. This was an ambitious undertaking, but I had spent considerable time guiding them through each stage of the writing process. By the end of the semester, some of my students had written remarkably cogent thesis papers, and I was pleased.

Ryan, however, did not complete the assignment. He handed in his original rough draft for me to check, and I pointed out that he had submitted a *report* not a *thesis*. He had not formulated a proper thesis statement, provided evidence of research, or composed a closing paragraph. I explained what he needed to do to correct his paper and gave him a week to hand it back in for a grade.

Ryan never turned in the thesis.

When grading time came, I was forced to give Ryan a "D" for his quarter English grade. I thought he would be upset, but I knew this was the grade he had earned. Ryan never questioned the mark and I assumed he was comfortable with the grade.

I was wrong.

Two weeks after report cards were distributed, my principal contacted me about a meeting with Ryan's mother. I was curious about the reason, but confident that whatever the issue was, it would be manageable. I respected my principal as a professional and honest leader, and I knew he respected me as a teacher. I was assured he would be fair and supportive.

The conference began with Ryan's mother entering the room, shaking hands with my principal, and sitting down without even acknowledging me. In that instant, I knew this would not be an ordinary parent-teacher meeting. Ryan was with her, and as he sat down at the table directly opposite me, his eyes were lowered and he did not look at me or utter a word.

As the meeting progressed, Ryan's mother accused me of being an irresponsible teacher. Ryan had told her I was disorganized and incompetent and that I had never graded his final paper or returned it to him.

"Ryan, I may be a lot of things," I said, looking at him eye-to-eye, anger rising in my chest, "but incompetent and disorganized are not two of them."

Ryan stared at the ground too embarrassed to even face me. I was flabbergasted, and every nerve in my body wanted to shout at Ryan and remind him how hard I had worked to make the course interesting and fun and how fortunate he was to be in the class. My heart raced, my face reddened, and my hands were perspiring. I had never before or since felt so unfairly attacked in a parent meeting. Instinctively, I wanted to defend myself, but I knew that would not improve the situation, so I somehow managed to remain calm.

I did not say another word.

The meeting ended when Ryan's mother demanded that Ryan's grade be changed to a "C." She stood up, shook my principal's hand on her way out, and once again ignored me. Ryan did the same. After they left, I stood there in astonishment and rage.

My principal, to his credit, told me that very instant he did not believe any of what Ryan's mother had asserted. This was not the first time she had complained about her son's grades, he told me, but he was afraid she would take these allegations to the board of education. He suggested that I gather all the written work Ryan had done on the thesis in the event she took her complaint any further, an action he feared might make my teaching life difficult. He assured me that I was an extraordinary teacher, but he would hate to see me go through any lawsuit she might bring. He pledged to support me whether I chose to change the grade or not.

I left the office feeling validated by my principal but dismayed by the decision I had to make. Changing Ryan's grade went against everything I believed in, but I knew that finding the corroborating paperwork was impossible. He had never handed back his thesis and I had no paper trail to support the grade I had given him. At that time, teachers did not make copies of student work, as is often the practice now, and I knew fighting this charge would interfere with attention to my other students. I felt helpless, so after much angst and soul-searching, I raised his grade.

This was the first and only time I ever did that.

The following year, each time I saw Ryan in the hall, he would avert his eyes and pretend he did not see me. It was evident to me that he knew what he had done was wrong. Often, I went out of my way to greet him in the hallway, but his attitude remained the same, and sometimes he even darted into a classroom and tried to hide from me.

I often wonder if Ryan really knew how destructive his lies had been, to *him*, not to *me*. His life that last year in high school was different because of that single instance of deceit, and I hoped he had learned the impact of not standing up to the truth. He was embarrassed and uncomfortable when he saw me, and that was punishment enough. I never talked to Ryan about this incident when he was in school.

Ryan graduated, and I lost track of him.

Time goes by, and sometimes teachers end up teaching children or grandchildren of students they taught in their first years of teaching. As circumstance dictates, I learned one day that Ryan's son was a senior at the local high school where I live. I first caught a glimpse of him at school when he and my granddaughter were both inducted into the National Honor Society. Ryan's son was also a talented soccer player who was being recruited by several colleges.

I did not talk to Ryan that night, but shortly afterward, a friend gave me his contact information and I sent him a congratulatory email. He immediately emailed back, told me how proud he was of his son, and said that he had married a Hereford girl. When he said her name, I remembered her, and I asked Ryan to please give her my best.

Ryan then inquired about me, and I told him about my retirement and my return to teaching as a substitute. *You can take the teacher out of the classroom, but you cannot take the classroom out of the teacher,* I remember typing. He responded "LOL" and that exchange of email pleasantries was our last contact.

I have often wondered if Ryan remembers that day in the principal's office when his mother had demanded the grade change. Did he manipulate his mother to complain about the grade, or was his mother behind the accusations? With a son of his own, did Ryan handle issues with grades or athletic situations any differently?

I would love to know.

As parents, our behavior speaks infinitely louder than our words. What lessons did Ryan learn from his mother that day?

BRIANNE

Great opportunities to help others seldom come, but small ones surround us every day.

Sally Koch

I taught Brianne when she was a junior in high school. She was a gifted student and a lovely young woman, and we became good friends. Although I was fond of many of my students, some stayed in touch after they graduated. The connection was personal in that they had shared their successes and failures with me when in school, and they wanted to continue the friendship afterwards. Others stayed in contact for a brief time, and then went on with their lives. In either case, I loved seeing where their life paths would take them.

Although Bri was rather quiet and reserved, her determination and integrity spoke clearly about her character. She did what she said she would do, and I knew I could always count on her honesty and leadership with other students.

The advanced health class having fun waiting for the bus to visit the assisted living facility. Bri is second from the right in the striped shirt.

In addition, Bri was an excellent athlete and played on the high school's county championship field hockey team as well as on the state championship lacrosse team. In my opinion, Bri was a well-rounded, smart, and confident young woman who would do well in whatever field she chose. I knew that I would miss her.

After Bri graduated, she attended a private college in Pennsylvania where she maintained a 3.6 GPA her freshman year. At the end of her second semester, Bri changed her major and transferred to Virginia Tech to study interior design and minor in industrial design. Virginia Tech had an outstanding engineering program, and she was excited about her new venture.

That August before she left for college, Bri came to my house for lunch and we had a truly engaging afternoon reminiscing about our days at Hereford and imagining the opportunities at Bri's new school. As I watched the hopes of this delightful young woman begin to take form, I was once again reminded of the blessings of my profession. When Bri left that afternoon, we promised to stay in touch.

Bri did very well her first year at Virginia Tech, and because some of her design courses were "hands-on," she asked if she could spend the day with my friend, who had established her own design firm, and had just completed working on some impressive properties in the Baltimore area. My friend agreed, and when Bri was home on break, they traveled together to visit several clients. Bri said it was an eye-opening and productive day.

Winter break ended and Bri returned to school. I did not hear much from her for several months. She was immersed in her studies and I was thrilled for her.

That spring, on April 16, 2007, as I was preparing dinner, I turned on the evening news and was stunned at what I saw. A student at Virginia Tech had gone on the deadliest shooting spree in United States history, killing thirty-two people and wounding seventeen more before turning the gun on himself. I stood still, unable to move.

And then I wept.

Fifteen minutes after I heard the awful news, the phone rang. When I picked it up, I heard the tiniest, saddest, quietest voice say, "Mrs. Euker, this is Bri. I'm just calling to tell you I'm all right and so are the other Hereford students who are on campus." Ten Hereford High School graduates were attending Virginia Tech. "I just thought you might want to know that none of us was hurt in the gunfire." My weeping escalated to sobs. I was so deeply touched that Bri reached out to me during such a devastating ordeal. I could not imagine how scared she must have been. I hurt for her.

We spoke briefly before we hung up, and I turned my attention back to the news.

Our Hereford High School graduates were safe, but other students who had come from high schools just like ours, were not. College students, who were simply studying for exams, trying to learn and pass their classes had been gunned down. I could hardly understand it all. The young man, who had destroyed so many lives in his rampage, had previously experienced emotional issues, but he had not received the care he needed. His mental state had disintegrated to the point that on that April day he chose to take the lives of other students before taking his own.

Because of this massacre, gun laws on campuses have been revisited, and colleges have taken steps to form assessment teams and implement emergency notifications as the norm on their campuses. However, the debate over gun control on colleges and elsewhere continues. At Virginia Tech, an entire campus safety section is included on the institution's homepage, complete with a letter from the president, emphasizing the university's concern for its community. Students can access it with one click.

For the thirty-two people who lost their lives that day, the changes came too late.

Bri graduated in 2010, and, after working as a designer, decided to change her career path. She began coaching women's lacrosse at the University of Colorado while working toward her bachelor's degree in nursing at Regis University. While completing her nursing practicum, Bri taught college nursing courses part-time. She also married her best friend, Chris.

Bri and I have emailed several times in recent years. Although I am surprised by the dramatic shift in her career path, I understand why. Some students have multiple talents, and often it may take experience and additional time to decipher which avenue to follow. I briefly considered that the tragedy at Virginia Tech might have led Bri to shift her passion. But in an email, she told me that after working as a designer for five years, she transitioned to a more meaningful and person-focused career. She said her career change had nothing to do with the shooting, but I still wonder.

I always told my students that their primary job in high school is to challenge their talents, to take the time they need to discover what they like, what they are good at, and find a way to contribute to their world through that passion. By way of encouragement, I often told them that I did not find my passion until I reached my forties and returned to teaching. It was only then that I uncovered the one thing at which I excel and for which I have the strongest gifts. Apart from my family, of course, it is teens for whom I have the greatest affection.

Over the years I have contemplated why I am so enamored by this age group, and I believe it is because I can see the hope, optimism, promise and vulnerability in them that many of us outgrow as we age.

In many ways I am like a sixteen-year-old. Although I am responsible, and complete the tasks of the day, my first thoughts in the morning when I arise are about how I can find fun, and I am always searching for the joy in life. I believe that this inborn enthusiasm is a true blessing even if it took four decades to find my avocation. I encourage students to search for their niche in life, even if it means considering other options from time to time.

The students with whom I keep in contact make such a difference in my life. As they search for their passion, they remind me that my passion matters too.

Yet it is the courage and resiliency with which these young people continue their quest, sometimes in the face of seemingly insurmountable odds, that is one of the characteristics I admire most in my students.

Bri's "small opportunity" in the wake of the Virginia Tech tragedy is indicative of the drive and kindness found in so many of the students who have passed through the doors of my classroom. They give me hope for the future.

When I think of them, I know that our world will endure.

*Bri and me on a recent visit
when she was home from Colorado.*

THE DIP

Kind words can be short and easy to speak, but their echoes are truly endless.

Mother Teresa

Hereford High School was known as having the third toughest high school cross-country course in the East and the seventh toughest in the entire country. The school is set in the gentle landscape of Northern Baltimore County. Because of the rural nature of the campus, no houses or developments are located within a mile of the buildings, and all of the students are bused to school.

Hereford's cross-country course is famous not just for its rolling hills and green valleys, but also for the *dip*. The *dip* is a twenty-foot chasm at the center of the course, requiring a fifteen-foot sprint across a bridge over a murmuring brook, and a daunting twenty feet back up the other side. *The course is a killer.* Anyone who knew of Hereford High School's cross-country facility had genuine respect for the power of this distinctive feature.

The Dip

Each year, Hereford sponsored the *Bull Run,* a prime cross-country competition. This run was a manageable 3.14 miles, but right in the middle of the course was the *dip*, and to finish the race, runners were forced to negotiate this treacherous, exhausting challenge on the way out as well as on the way back to the finish line. Teams from as far away as New York and Virginia journeyed to Hereford to compete in this race and test their mettle on the same course where the Maryland state final cross-country championships are held. This much-anticipated annual meet has always been a huge event in the Baltimore area.

The Dip
Hereford's Bull Run.

When I was in my forties, I was running regularly and had participated in several short and easy races in the Baltimore area. In my own mind, I was an athlete and in shape. The operative phrase here is *in my own mind.*

One crisp, warm, sunny Saturday, the senior class at Hereford was sponsoring a charity fundraiser on the Bull Run course, and invited students, community members and teachers to sign up to run. I taught many of the seniors, so I wanted to support them by running the race. Although this particular race was only a mile and a half, it *did* involve running the *dip* both on the way out and on the way back. I was confident that I was in pretty good shape and that I would be able to complete the course.

And so, I signed up.

The day of the race the sun was shining, the wind was gentle, and the temperature was a balmy seventy degrees.

I was feeling good. I was ready.

Most runners know that participants line up to begin a race in the order of their times with the fastest runners always in the front. However, as a novice, I wasn't clued into this particular cross-country protocol, so when several hundred people lined up to begin the race at nine a.m. sharp, my ADHD, firstborn personality led me to place myself right smack dab in front of everybody. When several people glanced over at me, I wondered, *Why?*

The starting pistol went off, and we began.

As the throng of runners approached the *dip* the first time, I was feeling comfortable, and assured myself that I was as competent and in as good shape as the other much younger entrants running alongside me. On the way down the hill I was fine, and even on the way up I was still feeling pretty good. However, I was not so much in the front anymore. I was more in the middle of the pack, but I thought that was good because I was still in the mix.

When we reached the half-mile mark and turned to return to the finish line, I again approached the *dip* with determined resolve. *I could do this.* Then I noticed there were only seven or eight people behind me. I had fallen even farther behind. Doubt crept in for the first time. *Perhaps I was not in such good shape after all.*

As I ran down the dip this time and began my way back up, I felt my legs screaming "How could you do this to us? We've held you up your whole life and taken you everywhere you wanted to go, and now you do this to us?" In addition, as I looked around, I realized at this point I was pretty much all by myself. Everyone else had finished the course, and the term "dead last" resonated in my brain.

I found myself exhausted and alone, with only a short distance to go to the finish line. Beads of sweat streamed down my back. Saliva covered my face and liquids spewed from my nose. As I clawed frantically at the wall of dirt to reach the top, I must have been a wretched sight. I began to question my decision to run this race in the first place. *I had done it for my students,* or so I thought, but *I was embarrassing myself. What were my students thinking? And more importantly, what had I been thinking to attempt this race?*

And then I saw him. At the top of the *dip* was Dan.

Tall, gangly, quiet, smiling Dan, one of my senior boys, an extraordinarily talented sprinter, who had placed among the top five runners in the county championships, extended his hand to me and I heard him shout.

"Come on Mrs. Euker. You can do it. Just a little bit farther. Keep on coming."

I reached for Dan's outstretched hand. After he pulled me to the top of the *dip* he said, "Let's run in together Mrs. Euker." As we crossed the finish line, the last runners to do so, everybody gathered on the sidelines clapped and cheered for us, and we all began to hug and congratulate each other. Even in my numbness and sweaty fatigue, I felt as if I had conquered the world. I high-fived Dan and thanked him for helping me complete the run. We all grabbed our towels and equipment bags and made our way to our cars.

Race over. Mission accomplished.

That race took place decades ago, and here's the thing: I know I expressed my gratitude to Dan that day for supporting me, but if I could see him today, I would tell him how much his kindness meant. The words of Fred Rogers, beloved host of the Public Broadcasting's televised children's show *Mister Rogers' Neighborhood*, come to mind. He said that his mother always told him "*What* really matters Fred, is helping others win too, even if it means slowing down and changing our course now and then."

Thank you, Dan for "*helping me win*" that day.

I can't guarantee that Dan would remember what he did the day of the race, but *I* will never forget. While his thoughtfulness might not have been a big deal to *him*, it was to *me*. I have been talking about this singular act of kindness for more than thirty years.

And, now I am writing about it.

ANTOINE

Don't judge my story by the chapter you walked in on.

Sinu Gurjar

During my teaching career, I often taught health in summer school to supplement our family's income, and more importantly, to encounter students from other parts of the county. Baltimore County has twenty-three high schools each with its own personality and strengths. I loved meeting and getting to know students from so many different socio-intellectual-economic areas, and because health was a graduation requirement, these summertime sessions were always full.

One summer I taught the five-week, three-hour-a-day course at a school near my home. When I saw the class for the first time, I was surprised. There were more than thirty students in the classroom, and it appeared to me that they were mostly divided into two groups.

One group was comprised of Advanced Placement students from one side of the county who were opting to complete their health requirement during the summer in order to fit the Advanced Placement science and math courses into their senior year schedules.

The other group was made up of mostly students from high schools on the other side of the county, many of whom had failed the course and were taking health the second or third time in an effort to graduate from high school.

This was an interesting and challenging mix of students.

The only student I knew was Armin, who was on the Advanced Placement side of the room, and who I knew to be an excellent student. His mother taught math at Hereford High School, and she was a good friend of mine.

From the first day, I adored this class. The discussions, particularly about sexuality and drug and alcohol issues, were lively and far ranging. While one side of the room was focused on attending an elite college after graduation, the other half of the class was well-schooled in city culture just trying to survive adolescence on the streets.

Midway through the five weeks, Antoine, a young man from the trying-to-pass-the-class-the-second-time group, asked me if I would be willing to write a recommendation for him. I taught seniors during the regular school year and writing college recommendations was a routine and comfortable task.

This particular young man had been a positive presence in health class. At times when I had needed students to settle down or when I asked for quiet to continue the lesson, I had appreciated Antoine's leadership, and I told him that I would be pleased to write the recommendation.

I asked Antoine to give me the name and address of the school to which he was applying, a name of someone in admissions, and a list of his activities as well as his grades. Antoine looked at me a bit embarrassed and said, "No, Mrs. Euker, I need the recommendation for my parole officer."

I was taken aback. I did not know any of Antoine's history, but I was impressed with his courage in asking me to write the letter. Recovering from my surprise, I said that I would write the recommendation, and I did.

Summer school ended, I bid farewell to the class, gave each of them a "goodbye letter," and a customary high five, and then went home to enjoy the rest of the summer at the beach with my family.

When I returned to school that fall, I noticed that Hereford's state championship football team was playing the school that Antoine attended, and as I knew Antoine played football, I told my husband that we should go. I knew that Hereford's team would probably trounce Antoine's team, but I was hoping to have a chance to see him again.

We went to the field that Saturday, and before the kickoff, I walked onto the football field to greet Antoine. He was leading the team in warm-ups, but when he saw me, he smiled, "Hi, Mrs. Euker. Can't talk now, gotta lead the exercises." I smiled back and strolled over to his coach to find out how Antoine's school year was going.

As we talked, the coach told me that Antoine was doing extremely well academically, and that he was also an unusually gifted athlete. As we spoke, I felt a twinge of guilt because our school had fifty players on our team and his school only had thirty. I was certain that Hereford would win, and I hoped our coaches would not embarrass Antoine's team by running up the score.

The game began, and I found out how wrong I was.

Antoine's football team was extraordinarily talented, and throughout the game, the score was awfully close. To my amazement, Antoine ran the ball into the end zone in the last two minutes to win the game for his team. What an upset for Hereford, and what a lesson for me.

Part of me was pleased with Antoine for scoring the touchdown, and the other part felt guilty for not minding that Hereford lost. I managed to find Antoine after the game, and as I had on that last day of summer school, gave him another congratulatory "high five."

I really was happy for him.

Not long after that game, I saw in *The Baltimore Sun* sports page that Antoine had received a full football scholarship to attend the University of Maryland. During the summer, I had met his parents, who were delightful, educated people, so I knew they must have been thrilled with this news.

As I finished the article about Antoine that day, I imagined how proud he must have been about his own hard-fought achievement. I remembered the leadership he had shown in my summer school class, and I shared a measure of pride. I would look forward to reading about him that fall when Maryland played football.

Four months later, on the same sports page in *The Baltimore Sun,* I read that Antoine had been arrested for assault and battery in an attempted robbery, and that he was in jail. The article revealed details of the incident, and highlighted his lawyer's comments. The lawyer defended Antoine saying that he had not been part of the robbery but had just been in the wrong place. He was not responsible for the assault or battery and shouldn't be prosecuted.

I really wanted to write a letter to Antoine's lawyer telling him about Antoine's demonstrated leadership in my summer school class. I thought that might help. But my husband dissuaded me, arguing that this situation was Antoine's mess to deal with, and that I had done enough.

I was distraught at how quickly a life can change because of a bad decision and I agonized over the pain Antoine's family must have endured.

As far as I know, Antoine never made it to the University of Maryland to play football. Even now, my sadness and disappointment for Antoine remain, and I must remind myself that strong people seldom have easy lives. It is in the moving on and readjusting that we manage to rise. Nothing worth much comes easily.

Perhaps that will be Antoine's story.

THE APPLE PIE AFFAIR

You are the average of the five people you spend the most time with.

Jim Rohn

Bob was the *extremely* competent assistant principal at Hereford High School in charge of discipline. In fact, many of the students and some of the faculty were intimidated by him and eager to do exactly what he asked. That commanding attribute is crucial if you are to maintain acceptable behavior in a school with more than one thousand students, and Bob maintained his game face well.

He could be especially terrifying to the younger students who were more easily affected by his strict demeanor. The older students, however, often came to understand his personality, and after they had graduated, respected his efforts to run a safe and orderly school. I not only appreciated, but also counted on Bob's willingness to act as *the bad guy* to ensure students followed school rules.

When I worked with Bob, he was in his early fifties, of medium build with a graying beard, and a head of hair that we knew had once been thick and wavy. Bob was also the most hyperactive administrator with whom I had ever worked, and he could also be extraordinarily *loud.* He had a twin brother and younger twin sisters, and when he talked about his childhood, I wondered how his mother had survived.

Although I had had several conflicts with Bob over the years, we had come to an understanding, and he had become a good friend. I did not always agree with him, but I deeply respected his work ethic and commitment to our students.

Hereford was the only high school in Baltimore County that offered a break for students in the middle of the day. This was called the *enrichment hour*. Students had a choice of participating in school activities after lunch or reporting to the auditorium to study or talk quietly until the bell rang. Of course, the auditorium attendance had to be proctored, so teachers were assigned several weeks during the school year to take roll and maintain discipline. This was a fairly easy task, and I never minded covering this duty because the enrichment hour allowed teachers to offer a variety of interesting activities.

Students Against Destructive Decisions (S.A.D.D.), the Gay Straight Alliance (GSA), as well as my Ophelia Club, a leadership development organization for young women— all clubs that I sponsored —were able to meet during that portion of the school day. Many students either worked at jobs or played sports after school, and those schedule demands made it difficult to offer an activity after three o'clock in the afternoon.

The Apple Pie Affair began on a normal Wednesday in October when I had auditorium proctor duty. I was working my way through the list of names and quieting students down, and as I turned my head, an object went flying past my right ear, almost hitting me in the head. Many students had seen what had happened, and an immediate hush filled the auditorium. I bent down and picked up the offending object, a packaged apple pie from the cafeteria, and looked at the students to figure out what had happened. My attention was drawn to some anxious shuffling amidst two rows of sophomore boys in the back of the auditorium, but I just put the pie down and continued recording attendance.

I waited to see what would happen.

As I continued marking attendance, a note was pressed into my hand. I unfolded the paper and read the hurried scribble. "Mrs. Euker, I am so sorry that you were almost hit. If I find out who did that, I will let you know. I love you so much." The note was signed, "Stacy."

Stacy was one of my junior girls who adored health class and who spent significant time in my room before and after school. Her family was experiencing difficulties, and I think I was her emotional support when she needed to vent. I liked Stacy and enjoyed the time we spent together. Lately, Stacy had begun standing up for herself with other students, and demonstrating self-confidence, and I was proud of this newfound trust in her abilities. I called her "one of my girls," and she just grinned. When I saw the note had come from her, I mouthed the words, "Thank you Stacy," and continued my roll taking. I thought the incident was over.

I was wrong.

Not long before the bell was to ring, the Assistant Principal Bob, stormed into the auditorium waving his arms and demanding in a loud, commanding voice, "I want to know who threw the pie at Mrs. Euker. She is the most valued teacher we have." I must have blushed a little at the over-statement. "We need to find who did this. She was almost hit. I want to know who's responsible!" He yelled and flailed his arms for several more minutes.

When no one came forward, Bob told students they were not going to class until he found out who had thrown the pie. I knew he had backed himself into a corner, because soon, new students rotated in for their enrichment hour and he could not keep these students past the bell. I wondered how he would manage this situation. I doubted anyone would *rat out* the guilty party in such a short time. But Bob kept at it. He thundered on and then three minutes before the bell rang, he finally told each of them to write on a piece of paper what they had seen. When the bell rang, the students handed him their papers before he let them go.

I headed to my next class. By the time I arrived at my door, students had already heard about the flying apple pie, and were atwitter. With righteous indignation, they promised to ferret out the offender and inform the office. One minute later my class phone rang, and it was Bob. By the time he had returned to his office, he had fifteen students waiting to give up the perpetrator. The identified student was sent to the nurses' office and Bob covered my class while I went to confront the young man. I could not believe the fast detective work.

As I walked into the nurse's office, I recognized the student as the younger brother of one of my senior girls. He stood as I entered the room and I extended my hand to him to put him at ease. He apologized and apologized and said the entire row of his friends intended to throw their pies, too, but at the last instant they had all sat down.

He had not. He had thrown his pie.

I sat with him for several minutes and we discussed ramifications of behaviors and what he might do the next time his friends come up with such a harebrained scheme. Not only was his act disrespectful but he could have really hurt me. He began to cry. I told him I appreciated his apology and I hoped he would think more carefully about his actions next time. I reminded him that friends are not always the best decision-makers, and that sometimes knowing when to stop was the smart thing to do. I told him that by the time he enrolled in my health class the incident would be forgotten. We would begin again.

As we stood to leave, I again extended my hand to him. But instead of shaking my hand, he hugged me tearfully, saying again how sorry he was. We both left the nurse's office together, his apology accepted. The following year when he turned up in my health class, he did well, and I enjoyed his participation in class. The topic of hurtling the apple pie never came up.

Both of us learned something that day.

All is rarely as it appears, and the Apple Pie Affair was my reckoning. What first was assumed to be a planned attack, turned out to be just a young man being pranked by his friends. Even though the pie posed a potential danger, the intent was not malicious. The value of taking surrounding events into consideration and investigating circumstances before acting on them was driven home to me.

I find that with teens, particularly, this "extra mile" or benefit of the doubt is crucial to helping promote growth. Perpetrators need to take responsibility for their actions, but just as importantly, teachers need to exercise patience, employ introspection, and on occasion, show kindness.

That was *my* lesson.

I have no idea how the apple pie incident would have ended had our bombastic assistant principal not taken charge. My guess is that nothing at all would have been done and the young man may have continued to exhibit questionable judgment. I do not know. However, I do know that he was truly sorry for his behavior that day, and he handled himself in a mature and repentant way.

His tears were *his lesson.*

BUMPER STICKERS

Choose always the way that seems the best, however rough it may be; custom will soon render it easy and agreeable.

Pythagoras

Because I taught human sexuality to eleventh and twelfth graders, it was crucial that the lessons were educational and age appropriate. I followed Baltimore County's curriculum guidelines closely and was comfortable with the subject myself. I enjoyed talking to my students about puberty, love and decision-making related to their relationships, and I found that creative teaching methods helped engage the young people sitting in my classroom in significant and serious topics.

Often in the very first human sexuality lesson, I sensed a bit of discomfort as I outlined the unit to my students. In an effort to avoid embarrassment, I insisted that my students follow two class rules.

The first rule was during discussions, if a student wanted to "pass'" instead of answering a question, that was fine, as long as it did not happen every time.

The second rule was that any questions asked were legitimate as long as proper terminology was used. To promote this last rule, I had my male students turn to their right, extend their hand to the person sitting next to them, shake hands, and introduce themselves by saying, "How do you do? My name is Penis." The girls were instructed to introduce themselves, "How do you do? My name is Vagina." I then asked students to turn to their left and repeat the introduction. By that time, students generally were laughing, and after the giggling and snickering subsided, they were more comfortable with calling sexual organs by the correct terminology.

Surprisingly, few students over the years invoked the "pass" rule.

Each semester a spokesperson from Planned Parenthood visited my class to talk to my students about the overall importance of using contraceptives, and I came to know the speakers well. The representatives from this national organization came with videos, charts, printed materials and examples of contraceptive devices as well as a sense of humor. I was impressed by their professional attitude and easy manner that enabled them to engage my students in discussion about such sensitive topics. Students continually told me how much they learned from these information sessions and how the comfortable atmosphere in my classroom allowed them to approach potentially embarrassing subject matter.

Only once did I experience controversial fallout from this lesson.

On that occasion, the Planned Parenthood speaker brought in a stack of bumper stickers emblazoned with the image of a large condom and the slogan "Just wear one." I knew I could not allow students to take them. Baltimore County Board of Education's policy guidelines were clear; we could show our classes the contraceptive devices and demonstrate how they were used, but we were forbidden from giving students anything to take home. I placed the bumper stickers on the back table, intending to put them away at the end of the class period.

Well, I forgot.

When the students saw them, they snatched up every last one of the stickers not knowing they were not permitted to take them. When I saw what had happened, I was *mortified.* In a panic, I rushed to the school office to tell my principal. I knew he would not want to be blindsided by repercussions from this delicate misstep. I imagined angry phone calls pouring in from offended parents complaining about the bumper stickers their children had received in school.

Mr. Jones, our new principal, was irate and reamed me out for five minutes in front of administrative assistants, other teachers, students and two parents. I was infuriated and humiliated as I slowly made my way back to my room to teach my next class. My face was beet red, and I was fighting back tears.

Immediately I made the decision to tell my incoming class what had happened and share with them how I had handled the situation with my principal. I knew I had done the difficult thing by telling him right away, and I wanted my students to remember that accepting responsibility for a mistake is of primary importance.

While glossing over my principal's unprofessional reaction, I explained the entire incident to the class, emphasizing that doing the right thing, although it might be the most uncomfortable option, is always best. In closing, I reminded the class of one of my favorite quotes, "Always speak the truth even if your voice shakes."

Before the students left that day, I asked them to do what they could to make sure the stickers did not end up on the lockers, the floor, the auditorium, the bathrooms, or anywhere else students might creatively attach them.

I was concerned about the unintended dissemination of the bumper stickers, but more than that, I was furious at my principal for belittling me in front of everyone in the office. I thought his behavior was demeaning, and I felt I needed to talk to him about his reaction to my admission. I could not meet with Mr. Jones that day, so I made an appointment to see him the next morning.

That entire evening at home, I was anxious about speaking with him and admitting once again to the fact that I had made such an unprofessional and embarrassing error. Other members of the faculty had warned me that because he was new to the school, he might not be easy to approach. He was unfamiliar with the environment of Hereford and the personalities of the staff. Still, I felt I needed to confront him.

The next day after repeating my apology to the principal, I used my absolute best communications skills to explain to him how uncomfortable and upset I had been by the scene that was caused. I suggested there was a better way the situation might have been handled. I reminded him that he knew my professional reputation in dealing with students as well as with parents was outstanding, and because of that, I had hoped he would trust me to handle this blunder. Although my voice was definitely "shaking," I was proud of myself for summoning the grit to speak in my defense.

I sat quietly and waited for his reply.

After a few minutes of painful silence, my principal stood up, and to my shock and amazement, apologized to me for his outburst. He shook my hand and told me what a valued member of his staff I was, and before I knew it, he gave me a warm, collegial hug, thanking me for meeting with him and raising my concerns. His reaction was so unlike what I had anticipated going into the office that morning that when I walked out, I was a bit discombobulated. To this day, my friends on the staff cannot believe that he actually apologized to me.

The personal vindication I felt that day has stayed with me, and I learned a valuable insight about courage and speaking up for myself. As difficult as it was to object to the way I was treated in the face of an admitted mistake, I did the right thing. In doing so, I garnered a new admiration for my principal, and I gained a new respect for myself.

Most importantly, I believe my students learned something, as well.

The bumper stickers never showed up anywhere.

JASON

Nothing ever goes away until it has taught us what we need to know.

Pema Chodron

Sexual assault and date rape are issues my health classes discussed at length. Teens' romantic relationships are more intense and serious today than in years past, and the pressure to have sex is stronger than ever. That pressure has intensified to the point where sex is often an expected part of dating.

In addition, the use of alcohol and drugs can lead to sex without consent or even awareness. Sexual assault and abuse have become serious problems for today's youth, and I believed that my responsibility as an educator was to arm my students with information—personal and legal—that could protect them from harmful situations.

And, so I did.

Whenever an abuse incident was reported in the local papers, I seized the chance to have students read the articles, re-examine their feelings about the incident itself as well as try to understand the long-term trauma that could result. These teaching moments were often the best opportunity my students had to envision the awful repercussions a single act of abuse could trigger.

Over the years, I counseled young women, who though trusting their boyfriends, had been hurt sexually, and I found that these couples were often average students who worked hard in school and had optimistic goals for their futures. One night of bad judgment had harmed them in ways they couldn't fully understand and had irrevocably altered their relationship.

I remember a popular, loving senior couple who were looking forward to their final months of high school before moving on to college. They attended the prom together and had made the decision to have sexual intercourse for the first time later that night. The following week, I saw the girl in the lavatory crying and I asked her what was wrong. Between inconsolable sobs, she stammered that her boyfriend had broken up with her. She didn't understand. Her expectation was that she and her boyfriend would become closer because of the sexual experience, but his perception was different. He told her he was moving on. Neither one was angry nor thought the night was coercive, but the result was heartbreaking for the girl.

Sex does not have to be violent or forced to be cruel. Sometimes it can just be premature, cavalier or misunderstood. Both boys and girls can suffer the consequences and carry the anxiety and overriding feelings of fear with them for a long time.

An even more harmful facet of teenage sexuality is the alcohol and drug use at parties and the unanticipated and disturbing sex that can occur as a result. In addition, popularity and a false sense of entitlement by virtue of wealth or physical prowess has given some teenagers a license for destructive behavior.

Years ago, an incident took place in which several members of an athletic team from an elite boy's school were drunk at a party and sexually assaulted a girl. They ended their rampage by pouring beer over her naked body when she was passed out. Compounding the horror, one of the young men took a video, and in his inebriated state, thought it would be a good idea to show it to his teammates so everyone could see.

Everyone did.

With the exception of eight players, the entire junior varsity and varsity teams were present for the sharing of the video. Some of the boys knew who the girl was, but nobody stopped the video, and nobody left the room. When news of the incident leaked out, the community was shocked and grief-stricken.

Not only was the school rocked by this monstrous behavior, but when the account of the attack made the local newspapers, the entire geographic region became involved. Some excused the behavior as "boys being boys"— shifting the blame to the girl "who shouldn't have gotten drunk." However, most condemned the boys' disgusting and demeaning behavior, and the harm done to the young girl.

Neighbors, friends and families were divided over what discipline should be meted out. The horrendous assault against the girl was a shattering experience for everyone involved, and the boys feared they would face harsh repercussions and the real possibility of legal prosecution.

The Baltimore County State's Attorney investigated to see whether criminal charges should be brought against several of the students, but no jail time was given to the boys. That precipitated soul-searching on the part of parents and children all over Maryland about the role of high school athletics, wealth and status.

The final judgment by the school was to terminate the team's entire playing season, which ended the school's chance to defend its state championship title. In addition, thirty team members were suspended from school, and the boy who had made the video was expelled.

These decisions were hotly debated.

Some argued that the punishment unfairly penalized players who had not participated in the assault. Several of the seniors had been awarded generous scholarships to attend prestigious colleges, and they were afraid that the schools would withdraw their offers when they learned of the incident. Family turned against family and friends became estranged over their views of the severity or leniency of the punishment. Few people had no opinion, and even fewer claimed the middle ground.

I was so angry at the entire situation. How could teenage boys be so pitiless and think such sadistic behavior was acceptable? It is still difficult for me to understand how these young men could be so violent and not know they were harming another human being. Some students who witnessed what took place that night were quoted as saying that they had a sense that what was going on was wrong, but the severity of what had occurred hadn't really hit them until the next day.

I did not know the girl, but I wondered how this young woman was ever going to move past this horrifying experience. In my dismay, there was nothing I could do except caution my students and my own children about going along with despicable behavior.

I supported the school's disciplinary action against the boys and was proud of the team's coach who was quoted in the newspaper as agreeing with the season-ending call, despite the lost championship opportunity. I wrote a letter to the coach praising him for putting honesty and decency above a championship trophy.

The following week, I made photocopies of the news articles and had my students read them, reflect on what had happened, and write their thoughts in their journals. Afterward, we hashed out their opinions at length, and I tried to understand my students' rather conservative and judgmental responses. Many were, in fact, merciless in what they thought should be done to the boy and to the athletic team. They agreed with the team's punishment, but most students believed that the boys should have been legally prosecuted.

I was encouraged by the students' astute thinking, their genuine outrage, and their subsequent willingness to share their own experiences. Several were familiar with the party scene and could relate to the incident on a personal level, and entertain the question: *What would I have done in similar circumstances?*

I was not surprised at what some of my students said that day in class. Although most thought someone should have tried to stop the attack or at the very least prevented the boy from making the video that night, given the power of peer pressure, they questioned who would be the one to do that.

Many studies show that kids are sexualized quite early, bombarded with sexual references and suggestive images on their phones, on television and movies, on Facebook, Twitter and Instagram, not to mention access to pornography through the internet. This saturated exposure to sex without context can desensitize malleable young people to the point that tragic episodes such this one can and do occur.

Over the years, I have often collaborated with outside community agencies to promote student learning. At the same time our classes were discussing this sexual attack, an essay appeared in the local newspaper written by a respected Baltimore writer about a similar incident that happened to him in high school. Without revealing specific details, he related how his school had handled the situation.

Dan Rodricks, the writer, then went on to congratulate the boys' school for its courage in enacting the timely and appropriate punishment. After reading Mr. Rodricks essay, I had my students respond to him, discussing his point of view and inviting him to come speak to their classes.

Mr. Rodricks accepted the invitation, and two weeks later, my students were treated to an hour-and-a-half interactive discussion with a professional writer about integrity, truth, being responsible for our actions and doing the right thing, always. He shared stories from his career in journalism and listened intently to my students' reactions. I was impressed not only by what Mr. Rodricks said, but more importantly, by my students pointed and introspective questions. Somehow, hearing these life lessons from Mr. Rodricks that day resonated with my students in a way they had not expected. What he said mattered, and they listened.

The story would have ended there, except that a week after Mr. Rodricks' visit, I was flabbergasted to learn from my principal that the boy who had been expelled from the private school would be transferring to our public school in two weeks.

Reminding me of the sensitive nature of the transfer, my principal cautioned me to treat the incident "with kid gloves." No one wanted any attention from the media about the transfer, and he implored me to do what I could to make the transition successful. I understood exactly what he was saying, but his request weighed heavily on me.

Having covered this real-life lesson in class, I was afraid of the potential prejudice my students might carry when they learned the identity of their new classmate. Could this young man ever be accepted at Hereford after the attention his story had received in my health classes? How badly had our open discussions poisoned the well?

Transferring to a new school mid-year can be difficult enough. Even under normal circumstances the disruption can be overwhelming and life changing for teenagers. I learned the boy had some friends at our school from playing recreation sports as a youngster, but after the reprehensible behavior he had demonstrated, I did not know how my students would receive him.

In addition, Hereford is a close-knit area and most students have been together in school since kindergarten. Their friendships were strong, and welcoming new people into their cliques was rare. I was concerned that given the circumstance this could be an even more difficult adjustment. In any case, I *knew* the transfer would not be easy for any of us.

Although I was still angry and troubled about the assault, I managed to inform my students that the young man was entering Hereford and relayed my fears about pre-judging him based on our discussions following the incident. I was afraid that having gone over the specifics in class that the students might hold this young man's past transgressions against him as he attempted to make a new start. To my surprise, the general feedback was that students, knowing what they knew about what had happened, believed they were better prepared to receive him in a more accepting way. Again, I was astonished by the maturity and insight my students demonstrated.

But I knew that time would tell.

And time did tell.

My students were accepting of the boy when he arrived. Most students, although suspicious at first, were willing to afford him the opportunity to make a new beginning. Within several months, he had assimilated into his new environment, handled the work well, and had become friends with some of the students who had been in my health class.

I was affected by my students' willingness to include in their social circles someone society had vilified. The thought struck me that *they* had been more accepting than *I* had been. My students' belief in starting over was evident, when mine was not. Perhaps discussing the incident in class *had* helped them when they were asked to entertain forgiveness, where I had only been able to harbor my disapproval of the boy. *They* were the reason *I* was able to begin resolving *my* feelings.

Once again, the teacher is taught by her students.

It did not hurt that the girls found our newest student quite handsome with a charming demeanor, and as an outstanding athlete, he helped our high school football team win the state championship that fall. Jason blended in quickly and with little incident. All in all, a necessary but painful growth experience for everyone.

Everyone that is, except for the girl who was so violently degraded. I have no idea how she was able to recover from such a vicious attack. I hope the transparency of this incident conveyed a message to young people that will prevent further abuse. Revelations through the #MeToo movement, and serious allegations aired during the Brett Kavanaugh U.S. Supreme Court confirmation hearings, have arisen because of young women who were willing to come forward even years later and revisit their trauma in an effort to help others.

I would like to believe that perhaps the girl in this case, is able to look back and acknowledge that *she* was one of those brave women whose courage helped create the change; that her strength in the face of such unimaginable brutality could be our strength, too.

For me, it is.

JILL AND AUSTIN

No distance or place or lapse of time can lessen the friendship of those who are thoroughly persuaded of each other's worth.

Robert Southey

That Tuesday was a dark day for the Hereford High School community. Rain pelted heads, and intermittent lightning and booming thunder contributed to the somber mood. The foreboding atmosphere was fitting. Grieving friends and family entered the church, greeting each other with tear-stained cheeks and loving hugs as they shared remembrances.

Austin had died.

Jill was there. She and Austin had been best friends forever. They were not really a "couple" as many high school students are. Instead, they were deeply entwined in a committed friendship. They were like family, and they watched out for each other, always.

Jill was pretty, smart and president of their class. Austin was active in several clubs, and they both were exceptional athletes. Jill was captain of the girls' field hockey team. Austin played football. Both were popular with classmates and had several close friends. Teachers and administrators respected them for their dedicated school leadership, and other students looked up to them. Jill and Austin were considered ideal Hereford High School students.

I do not remember exactly when things started to deteriorate, but Austin's grades began to slip the first semester of his junior year, and he often missed football practice. Both Jill and Austin were in my classes, and even *I* noticed a big change.

Gone was Austin's cheerful, helpful demeanor and easy class participation. His ragged hair skirted the edge of his collar, his skin was pasty, and he failed to turn in assignments. When he was in class, he had a distracted, faraway look about him. He began cutting classes, eventually skipping school altogether. Jill was particularly attuned to the beginning of Austin's downward spiral but could not reach him. She tried to keep track of him, encouraged him to make better decisions, covered for him so he did not get into trouble, and even wrote some of his papers for him.

But his behavior did not change.

Jill felt helpless.

Ultimately, Austin's disheveled appearance, weight loss, and foggy demeanor became his "normal." Teachers as well as other students offered support. As often happens with young people when we cannot understand them, we ascribe the changes to teenage angst. That is what many friends and the school staff did, hoping that time and maturity would one day return the "old" Austin to his family and friends.

The following year, Jill continued to excel in school, and was accepted at a large university in the Midwest. She spent her last year in high school, loving her classes, the many senior social activities and competing in the state championship girls' field hockey tournament. Jill was especially looking forward to homecoming activities and the dance that night. She and Austin were going together, and Jill thought everything would be all right.

But it wasn't.

Not only did Austin quit the football team two days before the state championship playoffs, but he also disappeared shortly after he and Jill arrived at the homecoming dance. She did not know where he went, and he never returned that night. Friends took Jill to the after party, and she managed to have fun despite her worry about Austin. After that night, Jill saw Austin intermittently throughout the year before she left for college.

They never talked about that night.

College was perfect for Jill and she enjoyed her four years there. Besides earning superior grades, she continued her athletic career, ultimately playing in several college division championship games. During her first year, Jill saw Austin at Christmas and in the summer, and although his behavior was still erratic, he left for college in Colorado the following fall.

After her college graduation, Jill became a teacher. At the end of that first year, Jill saw Austin when he came home from college. She remembered he seemed to be "clean," and she was happy for him. But soon he was hanging out with old friends who had been trouble before. Because of his fear of relapse, Austin returned to college early, but before leaving, he called Jill to say goodbye. Jill's family was having a party that afternoon, and because Austin was into his "old" behaviors, Jill would not let him come. She was angry and disappointed that he had relapsed *again,* and she told him she would see him the next time he returned home. Jill was losing faith in her best friend. She was heartbroken. Austin said, "I love you, Jill," and hung up.

That is the last time Jill heard from Austin.

He died three weeks later.

As soft music played over the funeral home's sound system, mourners quietly found seats. Austin's family sat in front, his mother, father and brother holding each other up as best they could. Jill's family was seated nearby. The two families had known each other for twenty years. Now they were sharing unimaginable sadness together.

Jill was the first to give a eulogy. She approached the front to say goodbye to her friend. Smiling, but stoic, she described Austin as a kind, happy person who loved the outdoors and liked to try new experiences. She spoke of their families' long relationship and the fun times she and Austin had growing up. Then she slowly reached into her pocket, brought out three small stones and showed them to those assembled, one by one. She explained that Austin collected rocks that had special meanings, and that he had given her these three sometime before.

The first stone was quartz, which Austin said was for balance. The second, an amethyst, was for calm, and the last stone was malachite, which stood for transformational tough love.

Jill ended her remembrance by explaining how each of these qualities was significant in Austin's life. While she spoke, the room was hushed save for barely audible weeping.

To this day, I have not heard a more touching and honest remembrance given at a memorial service.

It is never easy to say goodbye, particularly when a young person dies. It is not fair and we feel cheated when a young life ends prematurely. The question of "what could we have done" haunts us. A death is a loss not only for friends and loved ones, but also for the entire community. When tragedies occur, we do our best to move on in our lives by holding onto shared memories. And, we try to understand.

With Austin, we did not understand.

At the time of his death, some may have suspected, but most did not know, that Austin had become addicted to heroin in high school. After graduation when he left for school in Colorado, he and his friends lived in a cabin in the beautiful Rocky Mountains. At some point, Austin was in the wrong place at the wrong time and was killed during a drug deal.

He was only twenty-three years old.

Later, Jill transferred to Hereford High School and coached several girls' athletic teams. The faculty was thrilled to have their former student as a colleague. They welcomed Jill's involvement on school wide planning committees and valued her skills as a "technology guru" helping more seasoned teachers develop stronger computer skills.

Five years after Austin's death, Jill met and married David, a teacher and coach from a neighboring school. My husband and I attended the wedding at a resort in southern Virginia. The day was warm and balmy, and the wedding ceremony, overlooking the water, was highlighted by the inclusion of many of the couple's relatives.

Bright pink and lime green were the colors of the day in an atmosphere of unbridled joy. A handwritten note on the entrance table at the reception related that the money for Jill and David's wedding flowers had been donated to the American Cancer Society. Instead of an elaborate bouquet, each of Jill's attendants carried a single pink rose.

During the ceremony, a family friend remembered Austin with a prayer and a special reading. His parents were there.

I still see Jill from time to time, and we often talk of Austin. I always ask how his family is doing, and although he died more than fifteen years ago, I still see the pain etched in Jill's face when she shares stories about their time together.

She will always remember her best friend.

So will I.

TEARS

The world is filled with nice people. If you cannot find one, be one.

Nishan Panwar

My last year of teaching proved to be more challenging than I expected when I was asked to teach ninth grade fitness. Although I was certified in fitness, at sixty-five years old I was not the teacher my fourteen-year-old ninth grade girls wanted to have. The other teacher working with me that semester was a young, good-looking, charismatic man, and he was teaching the boys while I taught the girls. The problem was that my girls wanted the handsome, young, male teacher, not me. They resented the fact they had the great misfortune of being assigned to me, when they could see the attractive male at the other end of the gym instructing the boys.

The course was intended to improve the physical strength of the students through intense, planned fitness activities with pre-and-post-tests to measure their progress. Therefore, it was my job to plan activities that my girls *could* and *would* do to enhance their overall fitness. However, they elected to do next to nothing. They would loll around the gym, braiding each other's hair while gawking at the boys at the other end of the gymnasium, completely ignoring my attempts to interest them in fitness games.

At one point, I called the girls over, sat them down and in my strict teacher voice explained that I would plan any activities they wanted to enhance their fitness if they could give me ideas of things that they would enjoy that were "legal." This was my feeble attempt at humor, but only three girls giggled.

Sarah, one of the girls who resented me the most, had her hand raised all the while I was speaking. Most students will lower their arm until the teacher is finished, but not Sarah. She just kept her rude little hand waving wildly in the air the entire time. "*If* there is anything I can do to make this class more interesting," I said, "please let me know what it is."

I finally called on Sarah. "Can we have a new teacher?" Sarah asked in her flippant, smart-alecky, know-it-all voice.

The whole class laughed.

"No, Sarah," I said. "Just me."

The bell rang, and as I walked up the hall to my health class, I felt angry tears stinging my eyes. In all my years of teaching I couldn't recall a time when a student upset me so, and I was astonished by my reaction.

As I passed the weight room, I saw Justin, his arms flexed, demonstrating his muscular prowess for all to see. He had been my student the year before, and I knew and liked Justin. Although he was not an enthusiastic student, Justin managed to pass his courses and was on track to graduate with his class.

I shocked myself when I walked right up to Justin, and asked him, "Am I a good teacher?"

He saw the teardrops in my eyes, put down the weights and without hesitation said, "Mrs. Euker, you are the best teacher ever." To this day, I do not remember approaching a student in such an open and vulnerable way. When I look back, I realize I must have intrinsically trusted Justin more than I knew. And he responded in a caring and sensitive way to a teacher he knew needed support. That interaction changed the way I saw Justin as well as the way I saw myself.

"Thank you, Justin," I said, and with my chin a bit higher in the air, continued to my health classroom, wiping the tears away.

At the end of the following period, after a spirited and most interesting class with my health students, I was tidying up my desk before going to lunch, when I heard a knock at the door.

There stood Justin. He looked at me from across the room and said, "Mrs. Euker, you are the absolute best teacher I have ever had. Don't let anyone tell you anything else." I thanked Justin and he left.

Moved to tears *this time*, by Justin's unexpected kindness, I went to lunch smiling.

And Justin? Two days later, I found out that Justin was Sarah's boyfriend. They had been in a serious relationship and were planning to live together after graduation.

I often wondered if they ever mentioned to one another their interactions with me that day or made connection between a *callous unkindness* and a *compassionate response*.

JARED

Don't judge each day by the harvest you reap, but by the seeds you plant.

Robert Louis Stevenson

I taught Jared health when he was a junior in high school. Although he was popular and a gifted student intellectually, he did not work hard in high school and, therefore, barely graduated. Jared had a younger brother, Samuel, who shared the same intellectual ability, and who also did little to nothing constructive in the classroom. Rumors abounded that both brothers were in the "party crowd" and did their fair share of drugs on the weekends. Other than the whisperings of the rumor mill, I did not know much about the boys or their family.

Jared graduated, and I lost track of him.

Ten years later, after I had been retired for five years and had moved to a neighboring county, I received a call from Jared. Caller ID displayed his name, and to say I was startled to see the caller's identity is an understatement. I answered the phone and recognized his voice.

"Hi, Mrs. Euker, this is Jared. Remember me?"

"Of course I remember you, Jared. It has been so long since you graduated. How are you and what you are doing?"

Jared told me he was living in Baltimore, working for a wine and beer distributor and doing very well. He asked if I would be willing to meet him for lunch or dinner somewhere. After we chatted for a few minutes, I said I would be pleased to meet him. Jared proposed a trendy restaurant in downtown Baltimore, but I suggested a local café.

For some reason, I was not quite comfortable seeing a former student at such an upscale hot spot. Perhaps I was reading too much into his invitation, and perceiving more than what was intended, but I have always trusted *my gut* when it comes to questionable decisions. *My gut* was insisting on a less expensive, less stylish eatery nearby, so we compromised on a more modest and more public venue.

Jared was now an adult, but our relationship existed in the context of a high school health classroom when he was still a teenager. As anyone who works with young adults knows, teens can be very needy and vulnerable, and sometimes transference can take place. In psychology, transference occurs when feelings, desires and expectations of one person are redirected and applied to another. The relationship between teachers and pupils may be seen by the teen as closer than it is.

Because of the personal nature of sexual topics we discussed in my health class, I was attuned to the potential risk of breaching established boundaries, and despite genuine affection for my students, both male and female, I was always careful that my professorial interest in them was seen as only academic in nature. My boundaries were clearly defined, and I never experienced any questionable situations, but I could imagine that individual students might not see the dividing line as clearly as I did. Therefore, even ten years later, I wanted to be sure Jared and I were both on the same page about the context of our meeting, for both our sakes.

For some, this "church lady" approach to teacher-student relations might appear overwrought, but during my years as a teacher, I witnessed high school professionals struggle with inappropriate relationships in the classroom. The slight age difference between newly minted teachers just out of college themselves and their students, can cause problems. Even more seasoned teachers can be seduced by the adulation of their students.

Through the years, I heard gossip about teacher-student miscues, and faculty who had supposedly violated the standards teachers are ethically bound to uphold. The grapevine—laden with as much rumor as trust—just reinforced my sense of how difficult it can be to set boundaries with students, and ugly scuttlebutt served as a caution in my relations with them.

Eventually two of my peers *were* let go due to students' *charges* of sexual misconduct. In one case, the allegations were leveled years after the student graduated, and I saw how devastating those charges were for both the accuser and the accused. This particular teacher's two sons were students at Hereford, and after he left, these young men had to face their peers and other teachers every day. It must have been a humiliating and embarrassing time for them. Their father never returned to teaching, anywhere.

An unpleasant experience of my own had taught me to be cautious about Jared.

Several years prior, I found myself in a distressing spotlight when I was blindsided by an accusation rooted in a single student's intense dislike of me. Teachers and students are at the most basic level, just people. And people do not always like one another. Ashley was one of the few students who harbored resentment and tried to hurt me in the most hateful way she knew.

When I taught ninth grade fitness, Ashley was in my class for the second year in a row.

She had failed physical education the previous year, and as a tenth grader, was repeating the required course work in a ninth-grade class. Ashley was embarrassed and unhappy about this, but she had to pass the class to graduate from high school. And she blamed me for her misfortune.

Our relationship was further hindered by an incident earlier that year when I caught Ashley and her girlfriend in the parking lot after school taking off their shirts and exchanging them right in front of parents and buses picking up students at the end of the school day. The unwitting audience gaped in shock at the half-naked students. I could only imagine the flood of parent calls to the principal.

As I dashed toward the girls to stop them, my heart was racing, and I was sweating. When I finally reached them, they both said smugly they had no idea their actions were embarrassing or questionable. They thought it was entirely appropriate to walk on school property in their underwear. Unnerved, I reported the incident to the school assistant principal, and the girls were disciplined the following day. I do not know how many phone calls were received, but I do know after she had been chastised, Ashley was incensed and treated me with more disdain than before.

As the year progressed "adversarial" was the kindest descriptor of our relationship. Because trust is an issue with me, I was always wary of Ashley. Her antipathy toward me was apparent in her creative efforts to disrupt the class. I never knew how she would interfere in class, but I was certain she would always try. Nonetheless, she showed up for class each day that year and participated enough to receive a passing grade. I thought she had resolved her issues.

I was wrong.

Midway through the year, a parent meeting with all her instructors was called to discuss Ashley's poor grades. As one of her teachers, I was asked to attend. While the six other faculty members present offered their assessment of her performance in class, Ashley kept eyeing me while fidgeting in her seat and whispering to her mother.

Finally, I asked, "Ashley, what's going on? Would you like to say something?"

Ashley's mother then reluctantly reported her daughter had disclosed I had *touched her* in an inappropriate way in class that day. Ashley told her mother I had made her feel extremely uncomfortable.

I was floored.

With two specific words, Ashley had brought home every teacher's worst nightmare—the fear of a student's false accusation.

Color drained from my face and I looked at Ashley in speechless surprise and disbelief. Uneasy silence filled the room as my fellow teachers cast their eyes downward taking a sudden interest in their shoes. Ashley squirmed in her chair with a slight smirk on her face. I could not read the meaning, but my history with Ashley told me she was gloating.

She had won.

The moment passed but knowing the possible professional and personal repercussions of such a charge, I was flustered and unsettled. Recalling the reprimand Ashley received following the parking lot incident, I surmised the accusation of *touching* was a result of that anger.

Ashley was getting even.

The teacher leading the meeting had been a former student of mine and knew my solid reputation. He ignored the comment and moved on with other discussions.

The climate then was not as highly charged as today with heightened and justified anxiety about inappropriate touching. Although nothing came because of Ashley's claim in the parent-teacher meeting, I knew even as an innocent victim, I could have been released from my teaching contract.

When students make a charge against a teacher, their testimony is taken seriously, as it should be. And although I believe that sensitivity to student claims is an important and positive change in school policy, I do wonder how teachers are protected from false reports.

No one raised the issue again. Even Ashley's mother never reintroduced her daughter's accusation. At that time and during the immediate aftermath, I was more fearful than angry. The possibility of the tarnishing of my reputation and the debasing of my career as a teacher was sickening. I had worked hard to instill the concepts of integrity, honor and courage in my students. To face such a disgraceful allegation was unimaginable. The potential psychological damage to the students in my classes was as overwhelming to me as the personal damage to my own character. How could I expect my students to have faith in what I was teaching if I were perceived as not following the code myself?

The semester continued and seeing Ashley in class every day caused me to resent her more and more. In order to deal with that building anger, I ignored Ashley and concentrated on other students who were more receptive to me and interested in what I was teaching. I learned that positive responses could be found in class each day. I only had to be open to hearing them. And I was able to do that.

Ashley and I managed to skid through the semester without any further unpleasantness. I do not believe that she had any idea of the potentially disastrous reverberations her accusations could have caused.

Although, in truth, I do not think she cared.

I am still haunted by the potential harm to my professional reputation from this single accusation. This experience with Ashley may well have been the cause of my subconscious hesitation in advance of my meeting with Jared.

On the appointed day as I drove to meet Jared, I was still curious as to his reason for wanting to see me, and frankly, I was a little nervous. I even considered that this meeting might be part of a 12- step substance-abuse recovery program. Based on remembered comments about Jared's party habits, I would not have been surprised if that was his mission. I was even a bit unsure as to what to say to him, which surprised me as I am usually at ease visiting with former students. Seeing them happy and successful is one of the rewards of teaching and based on what Jared had told me over the phone, he was both.

I arrived ten minutes early and waited for Jared to appear. I smiled when I saw him walking across the courtyard promptly at noon. Jared was dressed in a suit and tie. He was taller than I remembered, and had darker, shorter hair, but overall, he looked the same. I saw a very handsome young man, and I would have recognized him anywhere. I greeted him with a friendly hug, and we went inside and sat down.

For the next several hours, I had one of the most delightful afternoons I had spent in some time. Jared told me that after high school he had found a job he loved. Because there is often an element of motherly pride when teachers see successful transformations in their former students, I was wholly engrossed in Jared's story.

He explained that he had started college but dropped out after one year and began building houses with Habitat for Humanity. He said he had made some mistakes, but as he put it, had "really learned about life." He returned to college, graduating from Towson University's creative writing program, and was presently studying for his master's degree part-time at The Johns Hopkins University. His current challenge was to do some in-depth writing about a subject that was significant to him.

Jared had chosen to write about his years at Hereford High School, and said he planned on publishing his novel at some point. He warned me that some people in the Hereford community might not like what he was writing. He then asked, timidly if I would read the more than one hundred pages he had completed thus far and give him some feedback. I told him I would be honored.

After chatting more about what I was doing, I listened to him tell me how much he had enjoyed the health course I had taught. This was a revelation to me, for I had no idea that he had even been listening to anything I had said in class. While I recalled his presence in the classroom, he had not been one of the students with whom I had a close connection.

As we prepared to leave, Jared insisted on paying the bill saying he enjoyed seeing me again. Jared also insisted on escorting me to my car, a worn eight-year-old, Toyota with dents in the sides. After thanking me again for meeting him, he told me I could expect his manuscript in the mail. We said goodbye and he walked away. As I pulled out of my parking space, I peeked with some curiosity to see where he had gone. I was shocked to see him get into a brand-new Mercedes.

The irony was striking. Jared was doing very well, indeed.

As I detailed the lunch with my husband that evening, I was still a bit puzzled by the whole experience. What was it that prompted Jared to call in the first place after such a long time, and why did he want to see *me*? Was this reconnection part of some personal "to do" list, or did he just want to have lunch with a former teacher. As I replayed our conversation in my mind, it was not clear to me whether Jared was really interested in having me critique his writing, or if he just wanted me to know that he was content and financially comfortable. I had no idea. To this day, I still don't.

Several days later, I received a brief email thanking me again for meeting him. Since then I have not heard a word from Jared.

And I never received the manuscript.

TEACHING OUTSIDE
THE BOX

I had to make you uncomfortable, otherwise you never would have moved.

The Universe

Often in education, we teachers are asked to teach subjects that do not fall within our field of study. And sometimes, we are even asked to instruct students in disciplines far outside our established content areas. These special assignments are allowed if the number of classes beyond the teacher's designated expertise does not exceed a set percentage of the teacher's workload.

Although these administrative requests are usually presented as *voluntary*, wise teachers accept the *opportunity* when offered. Not only do these challenges demonstrate a person's willingness to be a "team player," and commit to the success of the school, more importantly, saying "yes" to beginning Algebra when you majored in English literature can stretch the teacher in ways he or she could never predict.

A request to try something new can propel us out of our comfort zone.

I was asked to do just that one April when my principal called me into his office. After commending my work with the students and complimenting me on a recent article I had written for the local newspaper, he asked me to teach one class of eleventh grade English the following year.

Because of my essay, he knew I could write well, and because a large part of the curriculum required teaching students to write a thesis, he was confident I could "handle it."

He also pointed out that the selected readings for that grade level were closely aligned to the issues I already taught in my health classes. Astute salesman that he proved to be, this savvy administrator ended our meeting by praising my teaching ability and expressing confidence I would do a "good job." He assured me the students would love the class.

"Think it over and let me know as soon as possible," he said.

Although I knew the primary reason for his request was the shortage of English teachers for the following year, I was intrigued by the possibility of accepting the challenge. Writing a lengthy thesis had been a critical component of my graduate school experience, and I loved the selected readings for the eleventh grade curriculum. However, I also knew that teaching a new course would require a lot of preparation and the work would be overwhelming at times. Essentially, I would be a first-year teacher again.

After careful consideration, I decided to take on the task. Before that semester ended, the English department chairperson met with me and thanked me for agreeing to teach English and said he would do all he could to help me. He was an excellent teacher, and I knew he could and would give me the support I needed to present a successful class to my students.

I went home that summer and re-read some of the books that I would be teaching my classes. I wanted to be prepared.

When I returned to school the following September, I was dumbfounded. The English department chairman who had committed to helping me had transferred to another school over the summer, and a new chairman had not been appointed. No one was in charge, and the entire department was in flux. I had no idea what I was going to do. When I received my class list of English students, I literally became sick to my stomach.

Fortunately, one of the eleventh grade English teachers was an acquaintance of mine and after several meetings with her, I settled down.

She reminded me that I knew how to teach, and that mastering new material would not be as difficult as I imagined. She promised to meet with me weekly to guide me and offer suggestions on classroom management and creative teaching techniques.

I relaxed a little, reorganized my classroom, studied the English curriculum, planned my lessons, greeted my eleventh grade students, and... became an English teacher.

That first year teaching English turned out to be rewarding and fun. Although the work level and time commitment were intense, the student response was positive, and I learned a lot. I discovered *average* eleventh grade students' literary interests and began to select *appropriate* but *interesting* literature they would enjoy. Many students were "spotty" readers, and so my primary goal was to interest them in reading... anything.

I accompanied students to the school media center once a week, a spacious resource room where they could read materials of their own choosing. As I ambled around the center, I noticed students occupying the soft, comfy lounging chairs, or on the floor lying with their heads on their backpacks totally immersed in the pages of a book, or magazines on fashion, sports or cars and trucks.

This hour became *their* time.

In addition, each Friday, if students had worked well that week, I directed them to put their textbooks away, stand and stretch, and then sit comfortably in their chairs for the last half an hour of class while I read out loud to them. Stories written by Stephen King were their favorites, so I read chapters of *Night Shift* each week. When I stopped at the place where something scary was imminent and told them we would have to wait till the following week to find out what happened, they would howl and plead with me to continue. I always made them wait, a definitive lesson in delayed gratification.

Not once did a student put his head down and try to sleep, and that in itself was a success.

At the beginning of each new book assigned as part of the curriculum, I told the class I had a "guest speaker" I wanted them to meet. I then walked out into the hall, changed my garb to create a more authentic persona, and reentered the room, introducing myself to the class as the author.

For *The Catcher in the Rye*, J.D. Salinger slowly sauntered into the room with a leather jacket and flat cap on and a pretend cigarette in his mouth. Holden Caulfield was with him. For *A Raisin in the Sun*, Lorraine Hansberry twirled around in a 1950s skirt with fluffy crinolines as she pranced in to meet students. That day, students caught their first *glimpse* of Beneatha Younger, Hansberry's most memorable character. I believed authors describing their lives and discussing why they had become writers was more interesting to students than delivering traditional classroom lectures.

Some of the literature we read in class was challenging. *The Crucible*, by Arthur Miller, was confusing because in addition to the antiquated language, students had to know the history of the Salem witch trials. To help them understand the dialogue and story, each week, the class was divided into groups of five, and after twenty minutes of rehearsing, they acted out their portion of the chapter in front of the class. They had fun, but I also think students went away with a better grasp of the language and what Miller was conveying.

Half the semester was devoted to teaching students how to write. Composition of the thesis was a challenge, but as I walked them through the steps of formulating a cohesive opinion, many of them did well. Most students worked hard to do their best, and I was pleased.

One day, in an effort to take a much-needed break from thesis writing, I asked my students to grab paper and pencil, walk over to the windows of the classroom and peer out. Because the rural Hereford region of Northern Baltimore County features green trees, rolling hills, and pastures often dotted with grazing horses, the landscape is lovely.

View from the English classroom window.

I allotted fifteen minutes for students to silently jot down all they saw in detail, and when they were finished, they returned to their seats. I then gave them the rest of the class period to write an essay entitled *A Window to My World.* Their work could earn them up to one hundred points toward their quarter grade.

Students at Hereford often complained about their bucolic, pastoral surroundings, saying there was nothing to do on the weekends, and unless you had a car, you were "stuck" in the wasteland. They whined and belly-ached about having no fun, and rarely stopped to consider the advantages of country life. I wanted to see how they really felt, and I was hoping that sitting quietly and thinking purposefully would inspire them to see value in their surroundings.

I wrote five in-depth questions on the blackboard for them to address and told them to begin. The room was silent except for the scratching of pencils and pens against paper. I was anxious to read what they wrote.

As I reviewed the essays the following day, I was impressed with the details in their "window" writing prompts. I discovered that although many students still felt confined in Hereford, when I asked them where they wanted to raise their own families someday, ninety percent of my class said they wanted to settle in Hereford. Perspective for teenagers can be illusive to non-existent, and I was encouraged by their private thoughts. These seventeen-year-old students could envision that as adults, they might actually *appreciate* a quieter, calmer, more secure life and stay in Hereford.

And many of them did.

At the end of the school year, I was tired, but happy. My health classes had gone well, and I really believed that many of my English students had come to enjoy reading. One of the most rewarding comments I have had from *any* student in *any* class, occurred at the end of that first year of teaching English. I overheard several students in the hall discussing their teachers.

"Yeah, I got Euker for English, and, man, we gotta read every night. It's real bummer. If we don't do it, we will fail the quizzes she gives us. You should see all the reading homework we have. I can hardly get it done."

A left-handed compliment to be sure, but one much appreciated. As a left-handed person, I understood, perfectly.

Thank you to the universe for "making me uncomfortable."

MY FAVORITE LESSONS

There are no passengers on spaceship earth. We are all crew.

Marshall McLuhan

Several years into my teaching, I received a letter in the mail from the Walt Disney American Teacher Awards Committee inviting me to apply for the American Teacher of the Year Award. I was astounded, but also honored. I knew this award carried a financial stipend and some responsibility to share teaching skills and techniques with others, but I did not know much more than that. I did not know anyone who had ever been nominated.

As I read the letter, I learned that several people had nominated me anonymously. Although flattered, I was curious as to who had been moved to put my name forward and why. The letter attributed my nomination to a combination of student and community members' recommendations, but that was all the specifics it offered.

If selected I would be required to sign a contract to participate in a professional development program to explore innovative approaches to teaching and learning while developing strategies for collaboration and teacher leadership. I would have the opportunity to share my expertise with other teachers in my school and district.

In addition to letters of recommendation from several of my colleagues, my principal, and students, the application included four questions. The questions were about my teaching philosophy, classroom environment, favorite lessons and units, and what I considered to be the most critical elements of my classroom practice.

Because I had been busy "doing" and had not given much thought to these more philosophical topics, I had some introspection to do. As a full-time high school teacher, my energy had been focused on my students, not on me. Although I worked tirelessly to make my lessons meaningful, I had not taken time to consider these weighty questions.

I decided to apply for the award. And I began thinking.

Each school year on the first day of health class, I would always tell my students that health was one of the most significant courses they would take in their lives. My intent was to convince them that making honest, healthy decisions, analyzing their opinions and treating others with respect were just as important as reciting poetry or solving algebraic equations.

I ended this introductory lesson by writing the word "integrity" on the blackboard and asking what the word meant to them. I usually received various definitions, all pretty much on target, but I then suggested that integrity was *doing the right thing, no matter who is watching*. Rectitude requires maintaining a sense of courage and strength that allows us to look at ourselves in the mirror at night and like who we see.

I further demonstrated *integrity* by making fists, gritting my teeth, flexing my muscles, smiling and dancing around the room like a woman possessed, articulating the word *integrity*. The teeth-clenching and muscle-flexing were to remind students that integrity often takes fortitude and stamina, and the comical antics were orchestrated to help students understand that doing the *right thing* can also be fun. The students laughed hysterically to see a teacher act so goofy, and they left that day with smiles on their faces, and I hope a more defined idea of the power of integrity.

As I contemplated the questions posed for the Disney Teacher's Award, I concluded that the following lessons were among my favorite units to teach.

I believe students learn what they live, and meaningful lessons require relevancy and imagination for any positive change to occur. Students must be engaged in lessons as much as possible, and they need to see when immediate change occurs; the personal "aha!" moment is crucial.

For example, my students bid against each other in a "Values Auction" where they created their own fictional colony using a list of eighteen predetermined values listed on the blackboard. To obtain their own group's values, they had to outbid the other groups. Each group was given the same amount of money with which to bid, and individual mores and group values clashed as students worked out their differences to create their ideal society. At the end, each group was required to write a description of its society based on the values the groups were able to purchase. The groups then had to share their fictional society's ethos with the class.

Often, students discovered that certain societal qualities were more important to them than others, and that they could make their society work effectively by using one value to meet more than one community need. They learned to be creative and make adaptations where necessary.

Another activity I presented for the mental health unit was entitled IALAC, an acronym for *I am Loveable and Capable*. We are all born with IALAC —invisible "signs" that are with us always. As we grow up and face criticism, rudeness and hardship, pieces of our sign are torn away. Likewise, as positive things happen to us, pieces are added. At the end of each day what we have left of our sign, the ripped off pieces or the added ones, shows us what kind of a day we have experienced.

After I explained the concept of IALAC, I had my students make and decorate a personal IALAC sign. They were instructed to wear the sign for twenty-four hours and write a journal entry about what happened to their sign during that time. We then discussed the effect others have on our sign and how we can overcome the rips and tears that occur daily. We also celebrated the positive occurrences and theorized how we might help others repair their signs.

As an added assignment, I told my students they had to find my car in the school parking lot, and for five extra credit points, tell me the make and color. Students hounded me asking for hints, but I told them that with a little detective work, they would know my car immediately. What they found out as they pursued this puzzle was that my license plate spelled out IALAC.

When I first began teaching this lesson, I wrote the Maryland Department of Motor Vehicles and requested this vanity plate. I kept my IALAC license plate for many years through two subsequent cars, and even after my retirement. Many times, I would pull up to a traffic light, have the driver in the car next to me roll down the window and hear young people laughing, and yelling, "Hi Mrs. Euker IALAC*!*

My license plate continued to teach.

Hereford's S.A.D.D. Chapter demonstrating for parent responsibility
at the state capital in Annapolis.

Each fall we participated in the Death Watch, sponsored by Students Against Drunk Driving (S.A.D.D.} later changed to Students Against Destructive Decisions). During the Death Watch, selected students wore all black, covered their faces with white makeup, blackened their eyes, and with their teacher's permission, spent the entire day in silence. Each participant represented someone who had died due to irresponsible alcohol use, and on a large paper card hung around their necks, they wrote the name and death date of a victim of drunk driving.

Drugs and alcohol issues were a large part of my health curriculum, so I took part in the Death Watch, as well. Dressed in black with my face painted white, I made the commitment to remain silent the entire day. Using a tape recorder to pre-record the lesson, I "spoke" to students, gave them their drill, class work and assignments. Shortly before the bell rang for them to leave, I silently approached the chalkboard and wrote:

My father, Bill Cunningham died from
alcoholism in April, 1970. He was fifty-five
years old. I miss him every day.

As students left that day, many could not look at me, some fought back tears, and a few gave me a warm hug.

They had listened to the lesson.

Many of my classes over the years were designed to encourage students to maintain inner strength and be absolutely true to their beliefs, even if they are the only ones adhering to their standard. I knew that for teens, staying their course was an overwhelming task. However, I believed with practice and inspiration they could do it. Many of my lessons included unusual techniques.

During the human sexuality unit, boys and girls lined up on opposite sides of the room and wrote questions that they wanted to ask the opposite sex on a piece of paper. I collected the papers, and one at a time read the questions aloud to the appropriate side. Asking straightforward questions of the opposite sex about their experience and their view of their sexual relationships was an amazingly direct way to learn. Often the girls wanted to know about *erections,* and the boys asked about *menstrual periods.* Those classroom exchanges were some of the most deeply honest conversations I observed, and I hope encouraged students to understand one another better.

Each Friday, my health students wrote their thoughts, feelings and opinions about whatever was preoccupying them on a 3x5 card. I read the cards each week, commented on them, arranged them in chronological order, banded them together, and kept them until the end of the semester. Three months after my course was over, I mailed the cards back to each student with my comments reminding them of the commitment they made to themselves and the vision that was a part of their lives at that time.

I wanted them to remember.

Students in my advanced health class were required to keep a daily journal. Sometimes students recorded their general thoughts, but most often, they wrote about a controversial article or a video clip they viewed. Each Friday I collected the journals, added my thoughts, and returned them for the following week's entries. At the end of the semester, I collected the journals, and mailed them back to students after they graduated. My hope was that the responses students recorded while they were in school mattered to them, and that they would remember the important topics we discussed.

My overall favorite lesson related to the terrifying HIV/AIDS epidemic that was killing thousands at that time. After several days of informational lessons, I asked students to list twenty of their most important possessions and relationships on a piece of paper. Then I darkened the room, lit five candles, and read a story about a teen, who had contracted HIV.

As the teen became sicker, I detailed the things the person would have to give up because of the progression of the illness. Each time the person in my story lost something, my students had to lose as well by scratching something off their list. In addition, as I was reading the story, I blew out four of the five candles, one at a time.

At the end of the story, students only had one item left and only one candle remained lit. I asked students why it was so difficult to cross some items off their list, and then I asked them to consider why they saved the one they did. Finally, I slowly walked around the room, grabbed and tore up their papers with their one remaining item, and threw the pieces in the air. Tearfully, I reminded students that HIV/AIDS kills people.

They lose *everything*.

There is no choice.

The room remained quiet, but I felt an aura of nervous energy. Some students shuffled uncomfortably in their seats, not knowing how to react. Others sat very still waiting to see what would happen next. Most students were mesmerized.

I quietly stepped to the front of the room, turned on the tape player to Reba McEntire's moving song about AIDS entitled, *She thinks His Name Was John.* When the song was over, I looked students directly in the eye and gently said, "Please, please take care of yourselves."

I then blew out the final candle.

Students sat in the dark in stunned silence for several minutes until I turned on the lights.

I ended the lesson by showing a picture of the massive HIV/AIDs Memorial Quilt that was displayed on the mall in Washington, D.C. in 1987, and explained how loved ones who had lost a family member to AIDS created quilted remembrances of their loved ones and added their three-by- six-foot panel to the massive quilt.

Students then selected a colored square of paper and created their own *paper* quilt square celebrating their life, with stickers, lace, ribbons and markers. When they were finished, they placed their square on the class bulletin board to create our own "Living AIDs Quilt." This was a collection of each student's individual significance to the teacher, the class, their friends, their family and the world. At the end of each semester, I had each student take his or her quilt piece home to remember.

Before students left that day, they shared their feelings about the lesson and about HIV/AIDS. For homework that night each of them wrote a paragraph about what the experience was like for them. Some of their writing brought me to tears.

I also found humor to be an effective teaching tool. The slides of Sexually Transmitted Infections (STIs) were a perfect opportunity to demonstrate that.

Baltimore County provided a slide presentation to teachers that showed information about signs, symptoms, treatments and long-term effects of the diseases. When I presented some of the most distasteful images of sexual organs disfigured by awful diseases, students were generally grossed out.

When I came to the slide of a penis covered with so many genital warts that it was difficult to even identify the organ, I continued flipping back and forth to the slide while they begged me to move on. I reminded students that in real life you cannot just flip ahead if you become infected with genital warts, or gonorrhea or syphilis. STIs are serious and life-changing infections and taking care of oneself is crucial in *all* areas.

I told them that if they were at a party over the weekend, and they were thinking of making a *questionable* decision about drugs or alcohol or having sex, to pretend the devil was on one of their shoulders and I was on the other beating them on the side of their heads and screaming, "No, no, no!"

My students thought that was hilarious.

Over the years, I have run into former students who have told me how much some of these more graphic lessons changed their outlook. They took decision-making more seriously and thought about the results some of their behaviors might cause. In time, I learned that the way I introduced material in class changed students' ideas of who they wanted to be and the amount of introspection that was necessary to stay true to themselves, and I was inspired. Their self-discovery and foresight made teaching worthwhile.

I believed my passion had been realized.

Every Friday I gave my weekend speech.

"No drinking, smoking, drugs, sex, high salt or high fat, eat your vegetables, love your families, love each other (in a healthy way!), take care of yourselves, I love you. Look at someone across the room and when I count to three, yell 'you are good stuff' to them." Students did what I asked amid a clamor of laughter, finger-pointing and joyful weekend wishes.

I ended by saying, *"Go into the world and be amazing, because you can."* After laughing and some hugging, students left smiling for the weekend.

That is a pretty fun way to end a week.

And, for me, a truly fulfilling way to live a life.

Dear Susan Euker,

Congratulations! A number of different people have nominated you for Disney's American Teacher Awards, which honors creativity in teaching. This nomination demonstrates that your teaching has truly touched your school community. We salute you for your talent and impact on students. While we realize that you may want to thank the person who nominated you, **nominations were received anonymously** due to the young age of many of our teachers' ardent fans. We do not know who nominated you only their relationship to you (student, parent, etc.).

Disney's American Teacher Awards recognizes extraordinary teachers like yourself by giving you the recognition you truly deserve but rarely receive. Disney seeks to honor teachers who find creative ways to stimulate curiosity, engage the imagination and pass the joy of learning on to each and every one of their students.

Enclosed is a Disney's American Teacher Awards application for your review. We hope that you will choose to complete it and use it as an opportunity to reflect on your teaching. As well, we have included a letter for your principal, notifying him/her of your accomplishment as well as explaining a little about the program.

An independent committee of teachers and representatives from educational organizations will review all applications and select 30 teachers as Disney's American Teacher Awards Honorees for 2002. These Honorees will participate in a recognition ceremony in November 2002 in Los Angeles. All Honorees will receive a $10,000 honorarium, and their schools will receive $5,000. Ten Category Finalists selected from the 30 Honorees will receive an additional $5,000, and the Outstanding Teacher of the Year will receive a total of $25,000. The Outstanding Teacher's school will receive a total of $10,000.

If you are selected as a Disney's American Teacher Awards Honoree, in addition to public recognition and honor, you will participate in a unique professional development program. You will explore innovative approaches to teaching and learning while developing strategies for collaboration and teacher leadership. In addition, you will have the opportunity to share your expertise and insights with other teachers in your school and district.

Applications must be postmarked by **June 5th** and must arrive by regular mail— **no FedEx, UPS, certified or registered mail will be accepted.** We suggest that you review the entire application packet and immediately contact those persons who will write letters of recommendation [three letters]. In the past, teachers have missed the deadline because they couldn't get their recommendations back to include in their packets by the deadline.

We look forward to receiving your application for Disney's American Teacher Awards. Honorees will be selected and notified by October 1st by mail. Again, on behalf of The Walt Disney Company, we offer our congratulations on this very special nomination.

PS. Your name and the school's name are how we received the nomination. When you apply, any corrections you make will be made to our records.

Sincerely,

Terry

Terry B. Wick
Director,
Disney's American Teacher Awards

The application is also available on our web site, www.disneylearning.org.

The number on the label is a database number and is used only for tracking.

(ID: 21404)

500 South Buena Vista Street / Burbank, California 91521-0893 / 818-560-6900 Fax 818-560-3870

Disney's American Teacher Awards is part of **DisneyHand**, the worldwide outreach of The Walt Disney Company

IALAC

There is freedom waiting for you on the breezes of the sky. And you ask 'What if I fall?' Oh but my darling, what if you fly?

Erin Hanson

IALAC, I Am Loveable And Capable.

As teachers, we rarely know how what we say influences our students. That is a statement I believe wholeheartedly. Students just move on and we educators are left in the wake of their life's journey, wondering...

However, if we are allowed a momentary glimpse into our students' lives, sometimes the effects of our words may come back to us. And, if that happens, how lucky we are.

Carly and her younger siblings, Renee and Jackson, although graduating in different years, were dedicated students and for all the outside world knew, breezed easily through high school. I did not see them after they graduated, but assumed they were happy, successful and gainfully employed.

That is, until I saw Carly in the FedEx store twenty-one years later.

She came right over to me. "Mrs. Euker, do you remember me?" she asked. I smiled in grateful recognition, for in fact, teachers often run into former students, who they do not recognize. We remember a short, skinny, self-conscious young person, and may have trouble placing this tall, good-looking, formidable adult who is greeting us with an adoring and respectful gaze.

With Carly, that was not the case.

"Of course, I remember you Carly. You look exactly the same as you did in sixth period health class. I would recognize your smile anywhere. How are you?"

Carly was sixteen years old when I first met her. At that time, I had no idea what she was experiencing at home, and found her to be an intelligent, responsible student. She participated in class discussions and was well liked by other students.

When I taught the IALAC lesson, *I am Loveable and Capable*, I asked students to wear an IALAC sign for twenty-four hours and instructed them to tear off or add pieces to their paper, depending upon whether positive or negative things were happening to them. At the end of this two-day lesson, students recorded their thoughts in a journal. Carly did as I asked and at the end of the course received a well-deserved "A."

She graduated and I did not see her again until our fortuitous meeting in the FedEx office more than two decades later.

On that day, we chatted for a short time, and decided to meet for lunch. After sharing email addresses, we said goodbye, promising to reconnect. I left the FedEx store that day deep in thought, retrieving all I could from my overflowing memory bank about the Albert family, especially Carly.

When we met for soup and salad some weeks later, I was overwhelmed by this former student's story.

Carly told me that the IALAC lesson I taught all those decades before was the first time *anyone* had *ever* told her she was important. She went on to say that as an anxious, insecure, troubled teen, that lesson—IALAC *I Am Loveable and Capable*—changed her view of who she was. She began believing something positive about herself that she had never heard before. The dichotomy between how little she valued herself and what she heard in that health lesson was the one hundred eighty degree turn in her thinking that freed her to begin believing she was worth something.

She began to fly

Carly and her siblings were not who I believed them to be. They lived in a household plagued by addiction, and filled with physical, verbal and emotional abuse. Not only had there been physical beatings, but also emotional and corrosive rants that eroded the children's self-worth. All three children were continually reminded that they were terrible people and had minimal value. Carly's mother often told Carly how horrified her grandmother would be if she knew how Carly had turned out. Food was withheld, and if Carly wanted to have her friends over and make popcorn, she had to reimburse her mother for the treat. In addition, Carly's mother required her to pay a fee when her mom drove her anywhere.

Despite this less than idyllic childhood, the children became over-achievers and excelled at most everything they did. From scouting, to school-work, to athletics, the Albert children stood out. Carly told me that living in an addicted, abusive environment taught them not to ruffle feathers, to walk on eggshells, and to be outstanding.

All three Albert children attended college and graduate school, received numerous honors, and became contributing members of the community. Carly's sister became a well-respected family psychologist working primarily with addicted teens. Carly's brother, an Eagle Scout, who hiked the entire Appalachian Trail as a young man, earned his master's degree in international teaching, and taught in Bangkok, Thailand and Seoul, South Korea. Carly, after struggling with alcohol and drug addiction for many years, is five years sober and is a much sought-after internet consultant.

Listening to Carly's story, I continued to be astounded.

When she told me of the powerful impact the IALAC lesson had on her, I was reminded again of the power we educators have, to mold and shape our students. How we treat them and the messages we give them matter, sometimes in a life-changing way.

Often, we never know.

Carly related that as a teen, she had carved *I Hate My Life* on her bedroom door. Those etched words are now covered with paint.

And Carly is free to soar.

STUDENT TEACHERS

If your actions inspire others to dream more, learn more, do more and become more, you are a leader.

John Quincy Adams

One of the perks of teaching is the opportunity to influence young people who want to spend their lives working in the classroom. I believe, fervently, that "good teachers are born, not made," and during my career at Hereford High School, I had the privilege of working with some amazing student teachers who were just that. Interns from neighboring colleges came to me fresh, energetic and anticipating a chance to change teenagers' lives.

And they did.

As a master teacher, I subscribed to the theory of "baptism by fire." That is, the first week my student teachers were with me, they started by planning lessons, and little by little, they found themselves in front of the blackboard teaching the students. The "being in front of the classroom" was a bit daunting at first, but they adjusted quickly and learned to trust themselves as well as the students.

By the third day on the job, my expectation was that my interns would know each student's name and the classroom procedure. I explained my three "*Ls*" of teaching, *Learning* names quickly to earn students' respect, *Listening* attentively to their stories to promote trust and honesty, and *Loving* them through it all to cement a lifelong bond. Not all students accepted invitation to *bond*, but they were offered the opportunity.

Keri Hough – always smiling.

When I first met with my new interns to review expectations, I often learned that each student teacher had brought with them a special talent, and I encouraged them to use their gifts in their lessons. For example, one of my student teachers was an artist, and while she taught with me, she decorated the door and walls of the classroom with her colorful and creative artwork. In addition, she encouraged students to demonstrate their own talent as they worked on projects and assignments. That semester, my students became artists and my room became their studio. When that intern graduated, she taught health for several years. Later she focused on her own painting, becoming a well-respected artist, selling her works privately and in galleries.

Besides coping with the anxiety of teaching for the first time, another intern struggled with an eating disorder. When she taught the unit on stress and depression, she presented a moving and truthful account about signs, symptoms, causes and treatments for her illness. She became a positive role model for other girls in the class who thought they were the only ones suffering. That connection made an extraordinary difference both to her and to her students.

Because my student teachers were younger and more "with it" than I, students enjoyed having them teach. However, one of the issues that I sometimes dealt with was that the young, attractive female interns were only a few years older than the *a bit too interested* senior boys.

On one occasion, I was compelled to ask one of my interns to dress "more traditionally" when she was in school. Although her clothing style was popular and appropriate for settings outside the classroom, what she was choosing to wear was a little too suggestive for inside. She was receptive to my caution and began dressing more conservatively to minimize any distractions. Her creativity, knowledge of health issues, personality and professional presence were significantly beneficial to my students, and she became an excellent teacher.

Unfortunately, all of my interns were not happy teaching. One semester, my student teacher struggled not only to complete the university's requirements, but also to plan interesting lessons and relate to my students. Although she worked very hard to be successful, when she finished her time with me, my written evaluation was not strong enough for her to interview for teaching positions. She changed her plans and decided to enter the Peace Corps. The last time I heard from her she was doing well, and though at the time I am certain she was disappointed about not getting a teaching job, finding out what we are *not* meant to do helps us find our true place in the world a lot sooner.

Failure can be a blessing.

On another occasion, my student teacher was a handsome, smart, athletic young man and my students loved him. He was a hard worker and used his personality to his advantage with the students. In fact, after he completed his work with me and had to leave, one young girl was so distraught that she began acting out in the classroom. After some time and serious discussion about her feelings of attachment, she was able to let go and move on with her life.

Jonathon – positive role model for students.

I was fortunate to have met and worked with so many dedicated and knowledgeable young teachers during my career. Often, I would observe them interacting with the students and recall what it was like for me in my first classroom. I still remember my master teacher and several of the students I taught at New Oxford Junior Senior High School in Pennsylvania in 1962. That year made a significant impact on me, as that was the year Jewel Adams, after brashly critiquing my fashion sense, attested that *I had potential to become a good teacher.*

I wished the same for my own interns.

They learned from my students, and I learned from them. I liked being the observer and evaluator, and watching them morph into confident, interesting, devoted teachers.

Over the years, I learned that providing an effective and complete experience for younger teachers required more from the master teacher than just strategies on presenting effective lessons. Although I was strict about the work and preparation demanded of my interns,

Stephanie Mirabile – the students loved her.

I discovered the way in which I handled their successes and frustrations was just as significant as the teaching techniques I shared.

Kindness along with honest critical analysis of their work was crucial. I wanted my interns to leave Hereford High School knowing that they could be knowledgeable, firm and objective while teaching, but that ultimately, their students would remember as much about *how they felt when they were in the classroom* as *what they had learned while they were there.* Having interns understand that fine line between instruction and inspiration was my goal in training new teachers.

The relationship between mentors and new teachers is rewarding, but it is not for the faint of heart. My professional responsibility was to model a committed work ethic because teachers are mentally "in the classroom" twenty-four-hours-a-day, seven days a week for most of the year. I wanted my interns to understand that leaving school each day at the indicated time simply allows you to change your physical location. The psychological and emotional environment remains constant.

*Sarah Garcia, a former intern living in California,
who visited on a recent trip to Baltimore.*

Students become part of you. Taking on the challenges, joys and sorrows of young people is only for visionaries who are dedicated to transforming the lives of the next generation.

Mastering ones and zeros, engaging in high finance or scientific innovation all have their rewards, many with larger paychecks than what an average teacher takes home at the end of the week. But in keeping with the immortal words of teacher-astronaut Christa McAuliffe, who perished in the Challenger space shuttle explosion, *I Touch the Future. I Teach,* could there be a more exciting and wondrous life choice.

For me, there wasn't.

I hope for my interns, teaching was never regarded as simply a job, but rather a fervent avocation. My student teachers inspired my classes as well as me.

I remember them all.

SPECIAL PEOPLE

Every child is gifted. They just unwrap their packages at different times

Berta Lippert

Public Law 94-142 was passed in 1975. This pioneering legislation required schools receiving federal funding to accommodate the needs of handicapped students by providing them with fair and equal access to education. Federally supported schools were mandated to offer education for special needs students from birth to age twenty-one.

This law was a long time coming and much needed in our country.

Over the years, I taught many classes that included special needs students, but always alongside a special education teacher who was wholly responsible for the student. However, when I was a substitute teacher in a local high school after retiring from full-time teaching, I witnessed for the first time, the unwavering attention special students receive.

Until this point in my teaching career, although I had had some contact with special needs students, I had little idea of the depth of care special needs students require or any sense of the critical involvement of special education teachers and aides.

A high school, where I routinely substituted, asked me to be the lead teacher for a class with six boys with autism. Three paraprofessionals and two speech teachers would work with me. My lack of a special education degree prevented me from teaching, but I could support the special educators by interacting with the students and assisting when necessary.

Public Law 94-142 was clear about my role.

Because I was not certified in special education, the certified classroom aides gave me a heads up before the students entered the room about how the class would be taught, and I was told to watch the other teachers for guidance on how to assist. Mostly, I circled the room and helped students focus on their assignments.

What happened that morning was extraordinary.

The paraprofessionals devoted more than an hour rotating the boys from learning station to learning station, assessing their academic readiness in their particular area. At the conclusion of the rotations, the students returned to their desks to begin a brief period of relaxation and free time. During that interval, two students constructed towers with small blocks, another assembled puzzles, and still another listened to music on his headphones. A sixth boy played games on the classroom computer.

The room was silent.

Near the end of the rest period, one of the boys became self-injurious. He slid off his chair and started scratching himself while uttering unintelligible sounds. The four staff members sprang into action, placing him on the ground and gently restraining him to prevent any injuries. They worked with him for five minutes until the boy's body relaxed. Afterwards, I asked the para-educators questions about their process, and they explained their training in caring for students experiencing seizures or other medical crises. As they were talking to me, the same boy became self-injurious again, and the teachers repeated their intervention in a deliberate and calm manner.

Throughout the ordeal, the other students in the room remained at their seats and continued their work as if nothing were happening.

The student had three more self-injurious episodes before noon.

Each time, the teachers lovingly restrained and cared for the boy until he was able to return to his seat. The nurse and the principal of the school were summoned, and the boy's parents were called. The boy was taken to a special "quiet" room that was padded for his protection, with dimmed lights and no distractions, until his parents could take him home.

Two additional professionals came before lunch to help the remaining boys make brownies topped with bright green icing for St. Patrick's Day. Each boy took turns mixing the batter and added his creative touch to the iced squares. There was laughter and applause from us all as the completed delights were arranged on a plate for an after-lunch treat.

As I watched the day unfold, I developed a new and deeper appreciation for the special care some students require and was inspired by how these teachers and their counterparts in schools all over the country go above and beyond their teaching duties to meet their students' needs.

Being in class that day, I learned so much about the dimensions of addressing *all* students' academic needs, per Public Law 94-142. I was humbled to observe those *special people* who were the lifelines to education for the six students in their class, and, in awe of the many others who labor each day to guide their *special people* toward success.

Although I was limited in how much I could do to support those teachers academically, I *could* let others know of their commitment and enthusiasm for their students.

And I did.

I wrote the following letter to the principal of the school to convey my appreciation, not only as a teacher, but more importantly, as a parent who counts on exceptional care for every child in the school setting. I also left a detailed note for the teacher for whom I was substituting.

To quote my favorite bear:

"Some people care too much. I think it's called love."

A.A. Milne

Love, Mrs. Euker

SUSAN C. EUKER   1717 GATEHOUSE COURT   BEL AIR, MD   21014

Dr. Sean Abel

Principal

Patterson Mill Middle/Senior High School

85 Patterson Mill Road

Bel Air, Maryland 21014

Dear Dr. Abel   Friday, March 17, 2017

My name is Susan Euker and I taught at Hereford High School in Baltimore County for over 20 years. I retired in 2006, and since then, I have been substituting in the Harford County school system. One of the reasons I still like to be in the classroom is because of the students; they truly fill my life with energy and joy!

Today I substituted for Summer Zottman in the STRIVE program at Patterson Mill, and I had the most amazing day I have had in quite awhile. As I watched the deeply dedicated and loving para-educators work with the students, I was reminded of why I went into the teaching in the first place. Amanda Lenardson, Ronnie McCaffrey, Natalie Sieraki and Tony Protani treated the students with respect, discipline and care in a way I have not seen often in my career. Because one of the boys was having continual seizures, the para-educators were physically and psychologically challenged; the kindness and calmness with which they handled the boy were truly amazing. In addition to those teachers, two speech teachers, Kate Miller and Amanda Cambel were also present for some of the time helping with the activities. My favorite was the baking of Brownies with green icing (for St. Patrick 's Day!) which the students ALL mixed, poured and iced themselves (with help). We had a delicious tasting of our St. Patrick's treats after lunch!

In our world today rarely does anyone stop to appreciate the positive things that happen. I just wanted you to know that what I was part of today inspired me and taught me new ways of reaching students. I was truly moved by the care and devotion on the part of your teachers as well as the structured discipline of the students, particularly when the seizures occurred---the other boys sat at their table quietly and patiently.

Congratulations on the STRIVE program. I wish you and your faithfully, committed staff continued success in teaching these very special students.

Sincerely,

Susan Euker

Susan Euker   mimisu@comcast.net

CAROLINE

Just when we think we have our own stories figured out, heroes arise in the most unexpected place.

Cameron Wright, *The Rent Collector*

The day came when I eventually retired from teaching. This is a watershed moment in every educator's career, one that some teachers dread, and others have calculated down to the last hour of their last semester. I had turned sixty-five and could collect my pension and Social Security, but the most powerful driver was my desire to be with my family. The decision to retire was one of the most difficult I have ever had to make. I knew that I would miss my colleagues and students, but my daughters were starting families of their own and they lived nearly an hour away. The siren song of grandmotherhood was calling. My girls needed me.

When my first granddaughter was born, I left school each afternoon at three and drove to my daughter's house just to visit her for an hour-and-a-half. I then turned around and drove forty-five minutes through jarring rush hour traffic home to have dinner with my husband. I felt as if I were a rubber band, trying to stretch in two directions with my flexibility rapidly deteriorating.

After many long and serious discussions with my husband, we concluded that my retirement was the best option. At the same time, we also decided to sell our four-bedroom, two-story house and downsize from two acres, moving to a carriage house on one-tenth of an acre, fifteen minutes from each of our daughters. Having made this life-altering choice, I was surprised that I did not grieve over selling the home we had shared for more than thirty years and where we had raised our family. Instead, I looked forward to our new adventure.

My surprise retirement celebration planned by my Hereford students with balloons and Silly String.

To this day, I have no regrets about the move. With our children's invaluable help, we relocated to a comfortable and more manageable home. For a year, I was happy and busy with the arrival of my second granddaughter.

However, that was about to change.

Cruising through town a year after we had moved, my husband and I passed the local high school, and I saw students walking home with their backpacks, chatting, laughing and just enjoying each other. To my surprise, I began to weep.

"Susan, what's wrong with you?" my startled husband asked.

"I just miss being with high school kids," I answered between sobs. "I can't help it."

Although he did not fully understand my sadness, my patient husband, ever the problem-solving engineer, once again initiated an in-depth discussion about our future. I decided that I would return to the classroom, not as a regular teacher, but as a substitute. Knowing the boatload of work teachers do to keep up with their grading assignments, preparing lessons, coaching, serving on school committees, and remaining up to date on their certification, I *just* chose to do what I loved the most; being in the classroom with students.

I was confident I could handle classroom management, and that I knew enough to cover for most subjects, so I attended the countywide substitute certification meeting, learned the Substitute telephone call system, (SEMS), and requested my name be added to the substitute list.

I anxiously waited for the phone to ring.

Two weeks later I received my first call. The job was for a freshman Spanish class. I had taken French years before, but I knew no Spanish–*nada*. No matter, I took the job.

When the first class of students ambled into homeroom that morning, I was a little nervous and unsure of myself. I had not been in a classroom for more than two years and I knew things had changed during that time. The technology was more advanced and even taking attendance was different. With help from a student, I managed to complete my homeroom administrative tasks that day, and after the first period bell rang, with fluttering in my stomach, I waited for the class to enter.

I stood by the door to greet the students, and I realized that my heart was racing, and my palms were sweaty. When all students were seated, I introduced myself and told them my two rules: be punctual and be polite. Then I explained how to greet someone in a mature and mannerly way, reviewed "handshake" protocol and instructed them to introduce themselves to me. The students were not quite sure what to expect. You could hear uneasy snickering and the students' uncomfortable squirming in their seats. They must have been thinking: *Are you kidding?*

I approached the students one by one. They stood, looked me in the eye, and shook hands with me as they said their name. While the class did what I asked, the students were smiling, giggling and clapping for each other as they unabashedly enjoyed watching classmates complete this task.

After the students settled down, I told them I was happy to be in class with them, but that the only Spanish I knew was from the children's television show, *Dora, the Explorer*, "*Hola*, and *roja*." They laughed at my joke, and once I explained their assignment, they began their work as instructed.

By the end of that day, I knew that being a substitute teacher would be rewarding and fun. Although technology and curricula had changed since I had last stood before a chalkboard, I was reassured the students had not. They were still teenagers trying to do the best they could to fit into their environment. Even as a substitute, I believed I could help them do that.

Substitute teaching can be overwhelming at best and discouraging at worst. Not only do fill-in teachers have to contend with students they do not know, erratic schedules and classroom procedures that differ with each assignment, just navigating the halls and finding classrooms in an unfamiliar building can be daunting. I found most teachers' lesson plans to be complete and manageable for me as well as for the students, however at times the behavior of the class interfered with the success of the lesson.

Often students interpret the presence of a substitute teacher as a license to take the day off and tune out, and a few even enjoy taking advantage of the replacement teacher's unfamiliarity with classroom procedure. I must admit there were days I left the school frustrated, believing that I was an ineffective substitute, and swearing I would never go back to that teacher's class.

One of the worst days I had was with a math class, when one of the boys continually abandoned his computer assignment in favor of a gaming website. After warning him for the third time to return to the assigned task, I directed him to shut off his computer and go sit at his desk at the rear of the classroom; his time with the computer was over. He became angry, cursed and shouted at me.

When I ordered him to the principal's office, he stormed out through a door that students were not permitted to use. I followed him for a short distance to make sure he went directly to the school office. When I returned to the lab only moments later, I saw red, blue and green chewy candies strewn over the floor at the front of the classroom.

I was furious.

I did not know who had thrown the candy in my absence, but I told all the students to shut off their computers, return to their desks, and in a loud, exasperated voice, I reprimanded them for their immature, childish behavior. At the end of my ten-minute rampage, I declared how disappointed I was, noting they were in high school, not middle school, and that I expected better from them.

Their silence spoke volumes about their guilt. Some students had a difficult time even looking at me. When the bell rang five minutes later and the subdued students filed out of the lab, three girls stayed behind, apologized and gave me the names of the "candy hurlers." I immediately wrote their teacher a note explaining what had happened and that I would not substitute for her again. I finished teaching the afternoon classes with no other incidents, and as I left school that day, I handed in a discipline slip to the office.

I never wanted to be regarded as a mean, disagreeable, or cantankerous teacher. To me, those characteristics in the classroom are not only counterproductive to learning but can also inhibit student trust and respect. I always tried to be a positive role model for how to handle challenging situations, but my anger and feelings of failure this day stayed with me that afternoon and all evening.

I was still upset the following morning.

At six o'clock a.m., the phone rang, and it was the same school asking if I would substitute. When I went into the office to pick up my daily schedule, my knees went weak. The teaching assignment was for the same classes I had taught the day before. I immediately found the school administrator, told him what had happened in the previous day's class, and that the assigned work was way beyond my mathematical ability. He saw that I was flustered and upset, offered reassurance and sent me to the classroom with the promise he would send another math teacher to help me. I was still unnerved, but I did as he asked. The math teacher came, and I spent an amazingly comfortable and successful day with the same students.

Thinking back, I believe that returning to that class the following day taught the students a lesson about *resilience and not giving up*, especially on them. The one young man who had acted out the day before was absent having been suspended for three days, and that made all the difference, to both of us. I later taught him in other classes, where he was respectful and conscientious. I still wonder if I could have handled the situation more effectively. Or perhaps how I *did* handle it served as a catalyst for positive behavior in him. That certainly is my hope.

I was a substitute teacher for ten years, and this period was a most rewarding and energizing time in my life. I met many students who appreciated my role as a mentor, and more importantly, who gave me assurance that the future was in capable hands. During those years, I had only a few students who refused to listen, were disrespectful, or who broke school rules. When that happened, I followed school disciplinary policy and learned from those experiences as well.

I became comfortable working with creative, self-conscious, angst-ridden, sometimes blunt, and often challenging, contemporary bobby-soxers. I substituted each day with emerging confidence, but remained ever vigilant, as I knew something could happen on any given day.

And, one Tuesday in November, something did happen.

I met Caroline.

Seventeen-year-old Caroline was in my homeroom one Tuesday in November, and after I took roll, but before the bell rang, she stood up and asked for the classes' attention. When everyone quieted down, she announced she was going to have open-heart surgery the following week, and she wanted her friends to think about her. She explained that she had been born with a heart valve problem, and every ten years she had to have the valve repaired. She was six years old at the time of her first surgery, and now she was due for another operation.

The class was dead silent.

After the bell rang, several students went to Caroline, hugged her and wished her well. Before she left, I asked if I might send her a card. She gave me her address and squeezed my hand. Several weeks later, I mailed Caroline a note and a book I thought she would enjoy. She sent a return note reporting that she was doing well and that she appreciated my thinking of her. She expected to be back at school in a few months.

After her return, I only caught glimpses of her every now and then. Because this was Caroline's senior year and she was extremely busy with college applications, work and school activities, we did not have the opportunity to visit for any length of time. Caroline graduated and was headed to Messiah College in Pennsylvania.

That summer, after taking my pre-teen granddaughter shopping, we stopped at Friendly's restaurant for lunch. As we waited to be seated, Caroline smiled, walked toward us and gave me a hug. She was working as the hostess for the summer, and as she escorted us to our seats, she told us that she was so excited about going away to college. Her smile was dazzling as she spoke about her life, and I was so happy for her.

As we ate our lunch, I told my granddaughter all about Caroline, her surgery and what a brave young woman she was, trusting my granddaughter would be inspired by Caroline's story. When I asked the waitress for the check, she returned a few minutes later with a paper, but no bill. The note read:

Mrs. Euker, I hope you enjoyed your lunch. I would like to treat you and your granddaughter. Thank you for everything.

Caroline

Sometimes when I think of the overriding societal belief that teenagers are disrespectful, are on drugs, or are lazy and unproductive, I am painfully troubled. Even my own friends will say, "How can you substitute for high school students with all of the irresponsible behavior" and I consistently answer, "How could I not?" I am truly happier in the classroom with high school students than anywhere else except with my family.

I do acknowledge that the teen years can be trying for them as well as for society, but time we invest now to guide them as they grow pays off later. This is one of the joys of not isolating ourselves from the next generation. In the absence of contact with those who hold the future in their hands, we elders can become cynical and jaundiced about what is to come. I choose not to do that.

I have found that teens often become who we *think* they are. That is, if we *believe* they are smart, hard-working, productive, kind people, then that is what many will *try* to be. We also must take into consideration what our students have been taught at home and the unseen obstacles they face and try to create learning strategies that take their personal histories into account. The amount of time we have to influence our next generation is limited, but the "teaching moments" can be significant.

When I think about teenagers who have inspired me, I remember students like Caroline who embody the compassion, respect, thoughtfulness, integrity and courage that I often found among the students I taught. They are the young people who will make the world a more accepting place. Sometimes, as I adjust to life and the struggles and difficulties that are necessary for *my* continued growth, I forget that.

Thank you, Caroline for reminding me.

As I left the restaurant that day, Caroline and I embraced, said goodbye and promised to stay in touch.

And we have.

PEP RALLIES

Be aware of the place where you are brought to tears. That's where I am, and that's where your treasure is."

Paulo Coelho, *The Alchemist*

I can't help it. I am a sucker for teenage spirit, and I make no apologies.

One autumn day I substituted at a local high school, and as it happened, it was pep rally day. Now, I know about pep rally day, because I spent twenty years at Hereford High School with rallies every October on homecoming day. So, I was prepared for pretty much anything.

However, what happened that day was far from what I expected.

At the appointed time, I escorted my class to its assigned area in the bleachers. Once all my students were seated, I relaxed a little, and standing beside them observing all the excitement, was able to drink in the celebratory atmosphere of the event.

And drink it in I did.

Everything from the rafters to the railings was decorated in blue and black, the school colors, and the student dressed as the school's mascot, a black mustang horse, was charging around greeting everyone who entered the gym. Balloons, posters, banners, and cheerleaders flooded the gymnasium, and all the students cheered and waved like teenagers do when they have escaped the classroom for a brief period of time.

When all students were assembled, the band with its six drummers, marched into the center of the room, and everyone stood to sing *The Star-Spangled Banner*. Hanging from the end wall of the gym was a ten-foot American flag, and when the band played, and more than five hundred of us joined in singing the national anthem, it was too much for this old patriot. I began weeping as I sang and tried to inch back into the corner beside the bleachers so I would not embarrass myself in front of all these students and faculty me who had little or no idea who this substitute teacher was.

As we concluded with "and the land of the free," I managed to wipe the tears away and composed myself.

I often wonder why I become so impassioned by events such as this, considering my *advanced* age and the amount of time that has elapsed since I was a cheerleader and once part of celebratory parades myself. I know that the sound volume, roar of the crowd and general anticipatory excitement are part of it, but why the tears?

Was I yearning to return to that time in my life? Was this my chance to be a teen again, even if for a tiny moment, with no concerns save the final score of the football game that night? Was I just missing my youth?

Or was it a matter of simply loving the camaraderie and passion of teens in the throes of being festive in communal merriment; a momentary snapshot of adolescents reminding us all of a promise for the future?

The unexpected breather from a potentially humdrum day was a refreshing surprise for me. And I welcomed it with open arms...

When the roar of the crowd subsided, each fall sport's team was introduced over the loudspeakers as they ran through a paper banner with the name of the team painted on it in the school colors.

Again, tears flowed.

This was a spectacular celebration, in fact, one of the most organized and fun rallies I had ever seen in my years of teaching. The classes competed in games, held contests and even had the staff playing a "blind man's bluff" musical chairs game. The students laughed, cheered and hooted for their favorite teachers. Not only were all the students polite and respectful but the events were so well orchestrated that the entire assembly finished on time.

That, in itself, was quite a feat.

I really admired this high school for many reasons. The principal was visually accessible, and on most days, met students at the front door when they arrived for their "workday." In the early pre-school day buzz, as many teachers were in their rooms interacting with early arrivals, often light bantering and laughter filled the halls. The tone of the building was anticipatory; what would another day at C. Milton Wright High School bring? Students were giggling, sharing, planning at their lockers and preparing for that day.

In addition, many students excelled in their studies.

Several years ago, the students in the eleventh grade Advanced Placement U. S. History class scored higher on their national AP exams than any other school in the county. Kudos to their teachers and to the above and beyond effort of the students.

So many factors go into making a school *successful*, not only in the academics, but also in convincing young people to *want* to do well. Buying into *wanting* to contribute to their community and world in a confident and constructive way is key for students and staff if schools are going to thrive.

The principal's accessibility to students, dedicated support and hard work by the teachers and staff, a clear vision of what the school espouses and strong parent involvement in student and community activities are critical contributors to the *success* of a school. To quote the adage, "It takes a village," the village must be *mentally* committed, *physically* willing to work beyond what is asked, and *happy* with *who* and *where* they are.

In this teachers' opinion, the last two are the most significant.

My experiences at C. Milton Wright reminded me of my former school, Hereford High. The two schools are similar, with their rural, well-maintained campuses, and students who are generally respectful and aspire to excellence. The teachers and administrators promote school pride by offering many activities for students to further their interests. With fair and consistent discipline, I saw firsthand how student spirit promotes and reflects the respect for this great Harford County high school.

When the office called the following week asking if I could substitute, one day for German and another day for science, I didn't hesitate.

LOSS

Fairness does not govern life and death. If it did, no good person would ever die young.

Mitch Albom

As one would expect, devotion to adolescents leads to times of great disappointment and sadness as well as to times of great satisfaction. Given the number of happy occasions I shared with my students and their families, I also regrettably attended more students' funerals than I could have imagined. Each time I was saddened more deeply. I felt the loss almost as if they were my own children, because for me for a short time, that is what they had been.

Those sad moments were the most difficult to bear.

During my teaching years and beyond, I attended funerals of students who lost their lives serving our country, who were killed in automobile accidents due to inexperience or drug and alcohol use, who lost their battles to cancer or other devastating illnesses, or who died as a result of depression and suicide.

We lost two former Hereford High School students, Josh Snyder and Norman Anderson, while they were serving in the Middle East. In their memory, as an Eagle Scout project, a young Hereford student raised funds and created a small garden with a tree, a plaque and a bench near the stadium where both young men had played football. The Hereford community honored Josh and Norman with this tribute to their heroism and dedication to our country.

One of the most upsetting funerals I attended was that of Elliot, who had been on the badminton team, was a student aide for me, and who had stayed in contact after he graduated. In his senior year in high school Elliot became addicted to opioids, and three years later, overdosed and was found unresponsive by his roommate. Sadly, an all-too-common story in recent years as the opioid-heroin epidemic robs us of a generation of young leaders.

I knew Elliot's family, and was particularly close to his younger sister. The following year in school, seeing her in class each day helped me grieve my loss. I hoped our being together helped her as well.

These deaths of former students weigh heavily, and although the sadness softens in time, teachers who have experienced losing a student will attest that the sense of loss never goes away. Over the years, I have spoken either privately or publicly at funeral services, and as I shared the impact that student had on his or her peers and on me, I tried to recount incidences in my classroom. These little stories and remembrances bring solace to the students' inconsolable families, so I continue to share them.

Recently, I attended memorial services for two former students, both in their thirties, who left behind grieving spouses and children of their own. After each service, I was able to visit with the families and remind them of their loved one's school days. Even after all these years, I remembered where the students sat in my classroom and specifics of our interactions. I was able to share those memories, and I hope the words of someone who knew their loved ones as vibrant teenagers were a comfort to them.

I grew so fond of many of my students, that when they left high school, they really did not leave me. Because they were in *my life* for a significant period of time, they became part of *my history* as well. Often, I was included in their graduation celebrations, birthday parties, and weekend family cookouts. When I retired, one of my students and her family invited my husband and me for a "goodbye" dinner which my student had prepared especially for us.

I relished those opportunities to get to know my students and their families outside of school.

After I retired, sometimes with *my* grandchildren in tow, I met former students and *their* children at a local park to picnic and play. Additionally, I invited newly minted graduates to my home to visit and just catch up. I delighted in seeing my one-time students happy and doing well.

It was my custom when students in my classes graduated to give them a small paper with an image of a beautiful butterfly on it with the *words:*

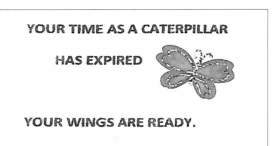

I was delighted in seeing them fly but was devastated when they did not.

And sometimes they fell.

I choose to remember my students seated in the classroom, young, fresh, energetic and curious, hoping to make changes they thought would create a better world. I recall in-depth conversations uncovering their thoughts and imaginings, the clever comments that made me laugh, sometimes uproariously, and the honest and vulnerable revelations some students shared that changed the way many of us saw things.

Those are the memories I carry with me. That is the picture I see.

The death of a young person is not the correct order of things. Often, we do not understand. We do the best we can to move on with our lives because that is what we are told is necessary. For many, that *moving on* demands time and unbearable pain.

But we try.

When young people die before their time, we lose a voice, the world loses a contribution to the future and a family loses an irreplaceable piece of itself. We cannot choose who lives, but we can choose to remember. As Marcus Tullius Cicero so beautifully wrote:

The life of those who die is placed in the memory of the living.

With my sense of loss lasting long after the funerals, I remember them all.

EPILOGUE

The most profound lessons we learn in the classroom are the ones we learn about ourselves.

Anonymous

When I was recovering from breast cancer during that cold, snowy, healing winter, and my bald, shiny head was covered with warm, soft, furry, hats, I began to collect my thoughts about teaching. I believed that the health curriculum I presented was life changing for my students. I knew the material was relevant to their lives, but I wanted to know for certain that what I had taught had affected their choices and shaped their futures.

My lessons were built around giving students the information they needed to make wise decisions about their health and well-being. And every Friday when my students left school for the weekend, I dismissed them with the affirmation *Go into the world and be amazing...... because you can.*

Even so, I longed to know that health had been an instrument of change and significance, and that my life's work was of value. I decided that writing about my classes would help me assess what had been accomplished. I craved the knowledge that following my educational calling had mattered.

The great irony in life is that what we think will happen sometimes does not, but something completely opposite and foreign to our expectation often does. Instead of one possible outcome, another eventuality shows up and surprises us, but ultimately fills in with ease and grace.

And we are better for the experience.

In O. Henry's charming Christmas story, *The Gift of the Magi,* a newly married couple is struggling to purchase Christmas gifts for each other when they have no money.

The husband decides to sell his gold pocket watch to buy his wife the set of fancy hair combs she has long admired.

A true gift of love.

His wife secretly buys her husband an elegant platinum chain for his beloved gold heirloom watch with the money she earned from cutting and selling her beautiful hair.

Another act of true love.

The irony, of course, is that neither expected the other to give up their most precious possession, and now they cannot use the gifts they exchanged.

On a practical level, the couple's actions are foolish because they are too poor to waste money on expensive gifts. On a deeper level, however, what they received is something they didn't expect: a more intangible gift that reminds them how much they love each other and are willing to sacrifice to make the other happy.

These paradoxical *shifts,* if acknowledged and welcomed, can change us in ways we cannot imagine. We can become who we thought we could not. Irony can teach us that.

That winter, I discovered irony while I thought and wrote.

In recalling my teaching days, I discovered that my students had taught me *more* than I taught them. I knew that my course had affected my classes, but I had not considered that the opposite would happen. *My students had changed me.* I became a kinder, more understanding, and more accepting, person. Much of what I wanted *them* to become, *I* became. I liked *my new* self a great deal, and, over the years, that new person continued to evolve.

I learned to be open to new possibilities and to trust that these opportunities are the foundation for growth and self-actualization as Abraham

Maslow wrote. These self-discoveries were eye-opening to me. *Who* was teaching and *who* was learning?

The irony was clear and definitive.

Last year, my husband developed cancer. This was a difficult time for my family and me as we cared for him during his illness. My children and grandchildren live nearby and were devoted to us both. They did all they could to help, but after my husband's yearlong struggle, he died peacefully at home. Many friends and relatives came to share our grief, and we managed to make it through that sad time.

A week after my husband's memorial service was my birthday.

I did not feel like celebrating.

That same week, Kelly, a favorite teacher at a local high school where I frequently substituted, asked me to cover two of her classes on that very day. Although I did not believe she knew it was my birthday, I decided that seeing her and her classes would cheer me up. I accepted her offer.

That morning, I walked up the stairs at 8 o'clock and peeked into her classroom. The room was decorated with birthday streamers and filled with smiling students all singing *Happy Birthday to You*. I was bowled over. Kelly stood in the middle of the room with her students, laughing and clapping.

Two of her students had baked a cake for me emblazoned with my signature message Go *into the world and be amazing... because you can.*

Zoe and Emma Peller with my birthday cake.

The students wanted to help me celebrate. Students I had cared for were now caring for me. I blew out the candles, cut the cake and we enjoyed a delicious respite in the school day.

A gift of love sprinkled with... irony

Later, Kelly invited me to come talk to her classes the following Friday about ageism, sexism, and long-term relationships. Her Advanced Placement Sociology class had asked for me.

Speaking to the AP Sociology class in the media center.

When I saw the classes that day, I participated in an educational and uplifting conversation with high school seniors who posed brilliant in-depth questions. As I shared my thoughts with them, I was aware again, that the learning was a two-way venture. I gleaned so much from them about the changes in social behavior over the years. Listening to them, I was struck by how different their world is from the one my generation knew. Life is more complicated now, demands far more of them earlier in their development, and forces them grow up sooner.

Kelly Machala and me.

Sometimes, when I listened to students describe their lives, I wondered if they had any childhood at all. With stories of family strife, separation and divorce, parents' job changes, fast-paced technology, crime and abuse, and high academic expectations, I wondered if they were ever able to run outside and chase bubbles, roller skate around the neighborhood, play *Mother May I?* or climb trees, ride their bikes to the park, play dodge ball on weekends on the schools' ball fields, hopscotch in their driveways or just sit quietly after dinner, licking a popsicle bought from the Good Humor truck before chasing fireflies at dusk. When I hear them relate their stories, often I am sad for childhood lost.

Maybe that is why I tried so diligently to present health in a relaxed and entertaining way. We laughed a lot in my classroom, and I hoped my students looked forward to being in health class. Some of the silly behavior I often exhibited was designed to let them know they could have fun in the adult world... if they missed gaiety as a child. They could choose what they wanted their lives to be.

In the end, I realized that my life was enriched more by my students than their lives were enriched by me. I do not want to discount the importance of my health course, because I tried extremely hard to be a consistently effective teacher. However, the totally unexpected reciprocity I experienced over the years was life changing.

Writing these memoirs is a love letter to all the young people who crossed my path, and particularly to those who stopped and stayed. Thank you for your honesty, your humor, your support and your love.

You have made all the difference.

Love,

Mrs. Euker

PUZZLES

No one knows everything, no one knows nothing. Everyone has a piece of the puzzle.

Lama Surya Das

One of the most important lessons I have learned from writing this memoir is how little I know. My understanding of the significance of life has been taught to me over many years by the puzzle-makers, who have helped arrange the collection of the often colorful, oddly shaped pieces of my life.

For many years, my life-puzzle had pieces that were continually added, taken away, and modified. Not much of me remained as it was. My puzzle expanded and contracted depending on who I met, what I saw, and the decisions I made.

That is the fascinating lesson of life; change is mandatory, but amid the joy, chaos and disruption, we often discover our hidden strength and can summon the power to continue. Puzzles are formed by the pieces we gather daily, and as we turn, tug and push, the puzzles morph into our personal pictures.

From my puzzle, blessings have flowed.

In this memoir, I have recounted how that puzzle-fitting process has changed me. Crediting my students for that growth has been the primary reason for my writing. Each one has been a piece of my personal, as well as my professional growth-puzzle, and I am ever grateful. Their work continues to this day.

I end my memoir by introducing you to some of the bright, perceptive, caring, witty and tenacious students who taught me the secrets of appreciating life's rich mosaic as the pieces clicked into place.

You know who you are.

Thank you.

CPL Joshua D. Snyder
2nd Battalion 6th Marines
X Co 2nd Marine Division

December 15, 1984
November 30, 2005

*The town of Hereford celebrating its 2020 senior class
amid the COVID 19 virus.*

A school is a building with four walls and the future inside.

Lon Watters

AFTERWARD

Sometimes the universe slides us love notes in the form of people.

Anonymous

Not too long after I completed writing my memoirs, I was cleaning out a closet in my home office, and I discovered a large box I had stored away many years ago. The carton was filled with letters from former Hereford High School students, from their parents and even a few from students in other schools where I had taught during the summer.

What a fun and emotional morning I had re-reading the thoughts of young people now grown and living their own lives. Many of these former students of mine are married, some have children, and most have busy careers. I almost felt like their grandmother opening a valentine or thank you letter for a special gift.

So many remembrances were awakened that day. Even after completing my stories, I realized so much more could have been written. A lifetime with teenagers permeated my soul, and once again, I felt the "joy of that small voice in my heart."

Nearly all the letters, notes and cards conjured the young faces of the students who had penned them, miraculously transporting me to long-ago classrooms and hallways I had not walked in years. Some of the notes made me smile as I recalled forgotten high jinx, silly moments and the echoes of laughter.

Others brought a tear.

In lingering over the heartfelt words, I realized some commonalities in what these students had written–a golden thread of teenage wisdom detailing what they appreciated most about their classroom experiences. In their own words, I am sharing fifteen comments from those letters about what my students liked best about their classes:

- Being in a warm and comfortable room with a knowledgeable and personable teacher who actually likes us

- A classroom where students are given opinions outside of the teacher's beliefs, can express themselves and are encouraged to think on their own

- A room that is like a warm smile that does nothing but make everyone who enters smile, and where students feel safe

- A classroom that is bold, colorful and full of life, just like the teacher, with comic relief sometimes that makes class fun.

- Quotes of the day and inspirational messages that trigger thought

- A teacher who is open and honest and spends time listening to ALL students and builds trust. Morning talks before class that "helped me survive"

- Class rules that we wrote ourselves, signed and posted on the wall as a commitment to each other

- A teacher with a positive, semi-contagious attitude that encourages students to discuss difficult issues

- The "pass" rule that lets us opt out of answering an uncomfortable question "because if students get too deep in a topic, there is always a way out"

- Leaving the door open for everybody and never hesitating to help someone in need

- A teacher in touch with her own being and those around her

- A warm, inviting room where there are inspiring stories, pictures of the teacher's family and former students, and sometimes flowers and candy mints

The entrance table to the health classroom.

- One who filled my head with important information, but also filled my heart with her love for teaching and her love for students
- Showing us it is okay to be the way we are and making students feel worthwhile
- Making things in life a bit clearer at a very confusing time.

I share these students' thoughts with the fervent wish that some of these components will become part of every classroom.

If we genuinely love teaching, then listening to students' insights may naturally lead to a more open and trusting connection. Understanding the teen persona is challenging, but looking back and remembering our own adolescent trials may help. It surely is difficult to believe we were all that young once.

Perhaps these revelations culled from this one teacher's rewarding career may inspire another cadre of teachers as they inspire the generation to come.

This is my hope and prayer.

BIOGRAPHY

Susan Cunningham Euker was born and raised in Baltimore Maryland. She attended Towson High School, received her B.A. degree in Health and Physical Education from Gettysburg College, graduating with the Frank Kramer Education Award, and earned her M.S. in Health Science from Towson University.

Over the years, she has taught state certification courses for high school teachers in sexuality education through Loyola and Towson Universities, and has been a conference lecturer on motivational health education techniques at Salisbury University and McDaniel College (formerly Western Maryland College). Her op-ed pieces have appeared in *The Baltimore Sun* as well as the *Los Angeles Times*, and her short stories have been published in *Readers' Digest*, *Chicken Soup for the Soul*, and *Heart at Work*. She has also written and reviewed curriculum for high school health education and system wide sexual harassment for the Baltimore County Board of Education.

Euker received the Stevenson University *Favorite Teacher Award*, (formerly Villa Julie College), the Hereford High School *Harbinger* senior class dedication, *the WBAL Television Class Act Award* for outstanding teaching and service, the Simon A. McNeely Health *Education Award,* presented by the Maryland Association for Health, Physical Education, Recreation and Dance (MAHPERD) professional organization, and the *Baltimore County Chamber of Commerce Excellence in Teaching Award.* She was also a *Walt Disney American Teacher of the Year Award* nominee.

Euker is now retired from full-time teaching, but often substitutes at several local high schools. She agrees with the 13thcentury Persian poet Rumi, who wrote, "Yesterday I was clever, so I wanted to change the world. Today I am wise, so I want to change myself."

She lives in Bel Air, Maryland near her three children and six grandchildren.